CANOEING THE JERSEY PINE BARRENS
Third Edition

by

Robert Parnes

An East Woods Book

The
Globe
Pequot
press

Chester, Connecticut 06412

About the Author

Bob Parnes was born in New Jersey and moved to California via the Panama Canal at the age of six months, only to return overland to the East thirty years later. His interests are numerous and varied. They range from mushroom hunting, which provides him with gourmet meals for his vegetarian beliefs, to physics, in which he holds a Ph.D. Fortunately for us, Bob's inquiring mind made him take up canoeing also, and it was then that he discovered the infectious pleasures of the Pine Barrens. For several years he led white-water and still-water canoe trips for the Appalachian Mountain Club. He taught mathematics and served as executive director of the New York–New Jersey Trail Conference. Nowadays Bob is living in the state of Maine.

Library of Congress Cataloging-in-Publication Data
 Parnes, Robert, 1931-
  Canoeing the Jersey Pine Barrens / by Robert Parnes. — 3rd ed.
   p. cm.
  "An East Woods book."
  Includes bibliographical references.
  ISBN 0-87106-491-X
  1. Canoes and canoeing—New Jersey—Pine Barrens—Guide-books.
  2. Pine Barrens (N.J.)—Description and travel—Guide-books.
  I. Title.
  GV776.N52P556 1990
  797.1′22′09749—dc20   90-31899
                                                        CIP

Drawings and photographs by Robert Parnes
Cartography by Andrew Mudryk from original drafts
by Robert Parnes and with corrections by Al and Fran Braley
Manufactured in the United States of America
Third Edition / First Printing

Contents

1. What This Book Is All About 1
2. Underneath: Layers of Sand 8
3. Human History 13
4. Beer Cans and Bleach Bottles 30
5. Pine Trees and Pitcher Plants 34
6. Animals You May Meet 49
7. When Your Bed Is a Bag 54
8. Rent a Canoe 59
9. Negotiating the Turns 62
10. River Descriptions 83

Wharton State Forest

11. Mullica River 90
    River Map and Chart 95
12. Batsto River 102
    River Map and Chart 108
13. Wading River 113
    River Map and Chart 116
14. Oswego River 122
    River Map and Chart 126

Northeast

15. Nescochague Creek 136
    River Map and Chart 140
16. Toms River 143
    River Map and Chart 147
17. Cedar Creek 157
    River Map and Chart 162

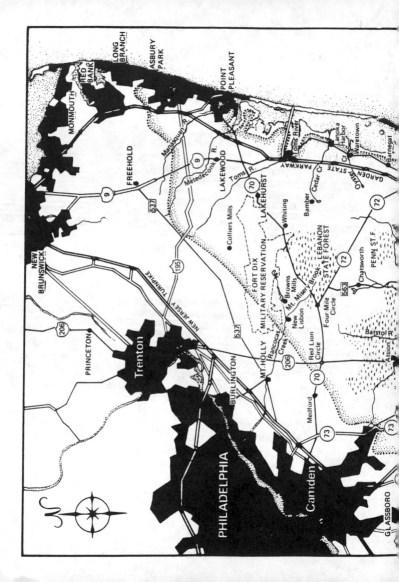

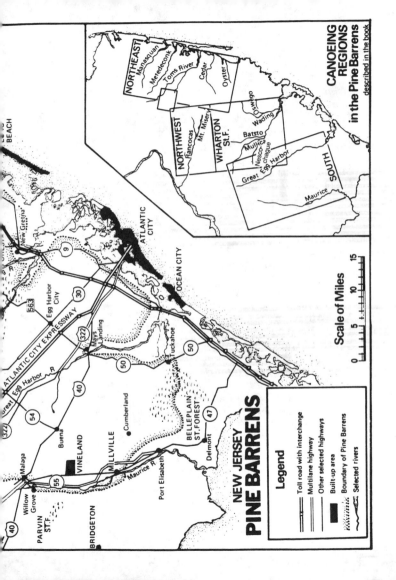

NEW JERSEY
PINE BARRENS

Legend

Toll road with interchange
Multilane highway
Other selected highways
Built-up area
Boundary of Pine Barrens
Selected rivers

Scale of Miles

0 5 10 15

CANOEING REGIONS
in the Pine Barrens
described in the book

NORTHEAST

Manasquan
Metedeconk
Toms River
Cedar
Oyster

NORTHWEST

Rancocas
Mt. Misery
Oswego
Wading
Batsto
Mullica
Nesco
Great Egg Harbor

WHARTON
ST.F.

SOUTH

Maurice

ATLANTIC
CITY

OCEAN CITY

New Gretna

Egg Harbor City

ATLANTIC CITY EXPRESSWAY

Mays Landing

Great Egg Harbor R.

Tuckahoe

Cumberland

BELLEPLAIN
ST. FOREST

Delmont

Buena

VINELAND

MILLVILLE

Maurice R.

Port Elisabeth

Malaga

Willow
Grove

PARVIN
ST.F.

BRIDGETON

BEACH

18. Oyster Creek   169
    River Map and Chart   172
19. Metedeconk River   177
    River Map and Chart   180
20. Manasquan River   184
    River Map and Chart   188

Northwest

21. Mount Misery Brook   194
    River Map and Chart   198
22. Rancocas Creek   203
    River Map and Chart   206

South

23. Great Egg Harbor River   216
    River Map and Chart   222
24. Maurice River   231
    River Map and Chart   236
25. New Adventures   240
    Lake Canoeing   240
    Seldom Paddled Streams   243

    Appendix A: Campgrounds   249
    Appendix B: Canoe Rental Agencies   253
    Appendix C: Medical Facilities   257
    Appendix D: Additional Useful Addresses   259
    Bibliography   261

1

~~~~~~

What This Book Is All About

The Pine Barrens comprise about 2,000 square miles in southern New Jersey, one-fourth of the entire state. They have a population density of only fifteen people per square mile, while the peak density for the state overall is a thousand times greater, and the state's average density is the highest in the country. Although most of the Pine Barrens are dry and infertile compared with the adjoining agricultural treasure land that has earned the Garden State its name, the area overlies an enormous underground reservoir of water. It supports few agricultural crops, yet two of them are so successful that New Jersey ranks among the highest states in their production. And despite the region's infertility, it sustains many rare plants and most of New Jersey's wildlife.

But that does not describe what the Pine Barrens are really like. First of all, they are a tangle of bushes growing in a lot of sand—all kinds of bushes, deciduous and evergreen; tall oak bushes and crawling cranberry bushes; and bushes with black, blue, purple, green, pink, red and white berries. The sand is white and yellow and reddish, sometimes clean and open, and sometimes covered with leaves, pine needles and twigs. Flourishing on this bed of bushes and sand are occasional fields of pine trees, thin and scraggly and unlike the more stately pines to the north, although they once looked similar. Here and

1

there, where the sand slopes down to the water table, narrow rivers wind almost endlessly, the tea-colored current moving sluggishly through jungle swamps of maples, low and open grass marshes, tall majestic stands of cedars and fields of pines. And everywhere, there are bushes. During spring and summer, flowers seem to bloom out of nowhere in the fields and open wetlands.

Secondly, the Pine Barrens are a recreation area for camping, canoeing, hiking and hunting. They are also a laboratory for geologists trying to unscramble various facets of land formation; for botanists locating plants that are rarely, if ever, found elsewhere; for zoologists looking for unusual insects and small frogs; and for ecologists relating all of these unique aspects together and evaluating the effects of any changes in the equilibrium.

Thirdly, the Pine Barrens are an interesting part of our history. They have provided wood for fuel and for building houses and ships, iron for the Revolution and for peacetime uses long afterward, and glass for windows, bottles and ornate ware. Traces of these industries can still be seen, modifying and overlaying the forest: crumbling dams downstream from open grassy meadows, ruins of old structures, bits of slag, alien trees surviving lost villages and old sand roads. Additionally, the Pine Barrens were a place of retreat, or exile, for a variety of Dutch, Swedish, British, German and Indian people, all of whom have contributed to the culture of the Pineys. More recently, the area has lent its soil to the production of cranberries and blueberries and to the quarrying of sands, clays and minerals. Also, it has become a home for increasing numbers of people trying to escape the congestion of the New York–Washington metropolis.

The Pine Barrens are each of these things somewhat independently, but each is also interwoven with the others.

Viewed independently, the most popular feature of the

2

Pines is recreation. To believe this, one need only try, on a summer weekend, to find a campsite in the thirty campgrounds serving the area, or to hire a canoe at the last minute from one of nineteen canoe rental facilities. Sometimes events get out of hand, like the time a friend of mine, while sitting on the bank of the Wading River, counted 700 canoes on that stream in one day. Some sections of the Wading can barely support two canoes abreast, so that day it was probably the most densely packed river in the world. According to an estimate made in the early 1970s by New Jersey's Department of Environmental Protection, an average of 3,000 canoeists visited the Pine Barrens on a weekend day during the peak season in 1970. By 1985 this number was expected to increase to 4,500 and, by the year 2000, to 7,500.

Canoeing is a sport that people of all ages and skills can enjoy, and it furnishes an efficient means for penetrating wilderness. The Pine Barrens rivers are interesting and fun, although they can be frustrating. Their widths vary from 3 feet (just big enough for a canoe to squeeze through) to 40 feet; the typical width is 15 to 25 feet. On the easy rivers the channels meander rather gently, but on the narrow and more difficult rivers the turns are sharp and close together.

Everywhere one is in intimate contact with the foliage growing on the banks and out over the water. Rivers that pass through swamps can lead to direct entanglement with branches and tree trunks, so a canoe must be carefully maneuvered along the sunless channels. Sometimes there is no choice but to scramble onto a log and haul the canoe over it to the other side. Elsewhere the rivers run clear and open: between the tall and stately cedars of bogs that twist through fields of grasses and water, called savannas, or past steep sand banks in fields of pines, where one can stop to view the scenery, enjoy a swim or walk through the forest.

The first book to describe the beauties of the river in the

Pine Barrens was James and Margaret Cawley's *Exploring the Little Rivers of New Jersey.* Published in 1942, it introduced many people to the Pine Barrens and other parts of the state as well. More recently, a second guide was published, *Canoe Trails of the Jersey Shore* by Joan and Bill Meyer. It is a compilation of articles that appeared over a period of time in the *Asbury Park Press.* I am indebted to this book for certain information that has made my own text more complete. Finally, the state distributes *Canoeing in New Jersey,* a free twenty-six-page booklet.

Well then, the reader may ask, in view of the present and anticipated crowding of the streams and the existence of three guidebooks, why a fourth? To this may be added the question frequently asked by people who find rivers they like described in print for the first time: "Aren't you ruining the rivers by telling everyone about them?" The answer to the first question is easy, but the second is somewhat controversial.

Answer one: I have intended that my book be more complete than the others. It not only describes more rivers but also discusses them in more detail and in a standard format that can be easily followed. It rates the rivers in terms of their difficulty. It has a section on canoe handling. And it provides background information on the geology, economic history and natural history of the Pine Barrens. Knowledge of these subjects increases the enjoyment of any canoe trip and one's respect for the general area. A lack of respect invites misuse.

The answer to the second question: It is true that rivers newly exposed to the general public stand a chance of being vandalized in some way. But the pressure of increased population dictates that these rivers will be "discovered" eventually, and without an adequate presentation they would be more likely to be mistreated. Rivers are, with few exceptions, misused not so much by canoeists but by noncanoeists who treat them as convenient dumping grounds. Such abuse is less likely

4

to occur if a river is canoed regularly and known to be popular. Furthermore, I believe that canoeists must assert their rights to streams or find themselves gradually squeezed into smaller, more crowded areas by the demands of urbanization.

As for the problems of crowding already taking place, the best procedure is to avoid them by canoeing at less-busy times: the early morning, midweek and out of season. One gentleman is known to lead canoe trips by moonlight, although it is precarious and about half the canoes capsize at some time during the run. Midweek canoeing may be impractical for certain people, but the other less-busy periods are within everybody's reach.

Take early-morning canoeing, for example. Although it may seem terribly masochistic to anyone who has not tried it, the pleasures far outweigh the discomforts. It is usually cool or cold, and there is often a mist suspended over the water. On colder days the oversize morning sun sends shafts of light through the mist that sparkle off the dew and frost covering the marsh grasses along the banks. Sometimes a light fog hangs over the ground, and the sun looks like a great creamy yellow ball diffusing light through the trees. In the fall the glowing rays enhance the yellow leaves of the sweet pepperbush and the red maple; one can stop at the riverbank in the midst of this glory to pick cranberries for breakfast. The stillness is broken only by paddles in the water or occasional ducks taking flight. Within an hour or two, the frost and mist are gone, the colors are normal and daytime sounds begin to break into the silence.

The seasons, too, have their own pleasures. Spring is full of flowers, unfolding leaves, high water levels and spectacular changes of temperature. One may awaken on a morning in April and find snow on the ground and a bitter wind blowing; drive to the river and have to cut through the ropes, now frozen, that bind the canoe to the car; and by late morning

5

paddle in shirtsleeves in the warmest of sunshine. Summer is a warm, relaxing time to swim and enjoy late flowers. Fall is crisp, clear, full of color and usually offers the best weather and the best chance of seeing animals. Winter is quiet, with evergreens standing out from deciduous growth. Sometimes there is snow on the ground and on debris in the water. But winter is best when the riverbanks and inlets are covered with a layer of ice. Then it is great fun to let the canoe drift into an inlet, crackling ice before it, and wait as the sound dies away and silence returns.

Naturally, each season has good and bad days. A crisp, clear day in January can be more comfortable than a cold, rainy day in August. When canoeing during the winter, one should wear warm clothing and avoid rivers that have an inconvenient burden of logs and other debris, as well as all frozen lakes.

Chapters 2, 3, 5 and 6 of this book furnish background material that has no direct bearing on canoeing, although it should enhance anyone's enjoyment of a canoe trip. The geology and economic history came mostly from books and journals. The geological history is controversial but reflects the most accepted current thinking. I restricted the natural history to my own observations, describing only those plants and animals that I have commonly seen while canoeing and which I believe an interested canoeist can find without great difficulty. Necessarily, these subjects are covered superficially. I apologize, but perhaps the reader may become interested enough to pursue them further by reading some of the reference material listed in Appendix E.

The river descriptions were drawn primarily from notes that I made, and secondarily from memories of my early years of canoeing. During the note-taking period, I canoed most of the rivers twice and some of them three times. The few that I paddled only once are so indicated. For this third edition, these descriptions were brought up-to-date with notes and information supplied by Al and Fran Braley, based on recent scouting trips and their previous experience.

The Pine Barrens are unique and should be preserved in their natural condition. I hope that my guidebook will make new friends for the region and that they will join people who already value the Pines in promoting that preservation.

The Globe Pequot Press assumes no liability for accidents happening to, or injuries sustained by, readers who engage in the activities described in this book.

2

Underneath: Layers of Sand

The processes that formed the Pine Barrens occurred in two major phases of geological time. Briefly, the first phase was the slow erosion of an ancient coastal ridge of volcanic mountains passing through what is now New Jersey, and the second was the deposition of sedimentary materials upon the ridge's bedrock, mainly by an invasion of the ocean. The first phase lasted nearly 400 million years and extended almost to the end of the Mesozoic era. The second phase lasted more than 100 million years, into the Cenozoic era. Time periods of such magnitude are impossible to appreciate, but perhaps some perspective can be gained by realizing that during the first phase the ridge of mountains eroded at an average rate of less than a thousandth of an inch per year.

The First Phase—Early History

In the early period of geologic history, the East Coast of the United States appeared completely different from the East Coast of today. The land that is now New Jersey was part of a long ridge of mountains that lay offshore of the ancient mainland, and the land that is now the Appalachian Mountains was a shallow sea that separated the ridge from the mainland. Streams flowing from the mainland carried sediments into the sea, and streams flowing down the offshore ridge carried sediments westward into the sea and eastward into the ocean. Slowly the ridge of mountains was reduced by erosion while the inland sea became more shallow. The sea withdrew and was replaced by a swamp that was inhabited by a dense growth of giant ferns and similar vegetation. Then, about 200 million years ago, the swampy sediments were gradually uplifted, tilted and folded to form the ancestral Appalachian Mountains.

These uplifted mountains began to erode, and streams carried sediments eastward. The ancient coastal ridge, by this time much lower in southern New Jersey, was still eroding, too. Meanwhile, northern New Jersey began to experience considerable volcanic activity. Huge cracks formed great basins there. Beds of molten lava pushed up almost to the earth's surface and created the Watchung and Orange mountains and the Hudson Palisades. Ultimately, about 130 million years ago, the erosion could not proceed much further, and there remained a gradually sloping plain, called by geologists a peneplane (from the Latin for "almost flat"), extending from western Pennsylvania to the ocean, which at that time was located considerably east of the present New Jersey coast. The peneplane consisted of the bedrock of the worn-down offshore ridge and layers of sand, gravel and clay deposited on it by the Appalachian streams. The streams, ancestors of the Delaware and Schuylkill rivers, flowed directly southeast across New Jersey and into the ocean. In southern New Jersey and to the south along the East Coast, the peneplane was the foundation for today's coastal plain.

The Second Phase—Creation of the Pine Barrens

The Pine Barrens were formed by small fluctuations in a delicate balance of powerful forces. The combatants were the rivers, which carried sediments from the Appalachian Moun-

9

tains, and the ocean, which carried marine sediments. The ocean advanced and withdrew repeatedly over the peneplane. As it did, the interface between it and the rivers, made up of swamps, deltas, mud flats and lagoons, slowly moved to and fro. Sediments were deposited there by the ocean, the rivers or both.

The first advance of the ocean occurred when the Appalachian Mountains began to arch very gently, causing the peneplane to tilt to the east. This increased the activity of the eroding streams so that they carried more sediments into the coastal region. The ocean spread over New Jersey and into Pennsylvania. It shifted back and forth at least eleven times, and each time it distributed the sediments deposited by the streams. (One of the sedimentary layers, which measures up to several hundred feet thick and is composed chiefly of clay, is exposed along Raritan Bay; it has provided material for the manufacture of bricks, porcelain and pottery.) Eventually, the land rose slightly, and the ocean withdrew. Temperatures were warmer than they are now. Dinosaurs, on the verge of extinction, lived in marshes and swamps along the edge of the fluctuating ocean. Flowering plants and deciduous trees evolved; sassafras and magnolia grew alongside conifers and fern trees. The Rocky Mountains were rising in the West. It was the end of the age of giant reptiles and the beginning of the age of mammals, about 70 million years ago.

On its next advance, the ocean again oscillated over a period of several tens of millions of years before withdrawing far beyond the present coastline. It left behind sediments of sand and clay in varying compositions. Some of them formed greensand, a rock of clay, and glauconite, which is a green-colored mineral rich in iron. (Today, outcroppings of glauconite can be seen on the western edge of the Pine Barrens at Medford and Vincentown. It was a source of bog iron and was used until recently as a soil conditioner and water softener.) During this

10

period crocodiles lived along the shifting coastline, and grasses and fruit trees continued to evolve.

About 25 million years ago, the Appalachian Mountains began to arch gently for the second time, and the ocean advanced once again, but not as far as before. When it retreated it left behind sediments of finely grained minerals and sand. On its last advance it covered southern New Jersey. At that time the Appalachians were higher, and the more active streams carried coarser sediments down onto the plains and deposited them in front of the advancing ocean. This layer represents the climax in the formation of the Pine Barrens. It is known as the Cohansey Formation, named after outcroppings on the banks of Cohansey Creek in Cumberland County. (The creek, in turn, was named after Chief Cohansick of the Lenni Lenape Indians.) In some places the Cohansey Formation is more than 200 feet thick.

As the ocean retreated, rivers poured down from the rising Appalachian Mountains and deposited a layer of coarse gravel and pebbles. (Called the Beacon Hill Formation, most of the layer has since eroded away, but traces can still be found on hills in Monmouth, Burlington and Ocean counties—notably on Beacon Hill in Monmouth County and Apple Pie Hill in the Pine Barrens.) Some time after this, the Delaware and Schuylkill rivers were diverted to their present southwesterly flows, and the Pine Barrens region formed a new drainage system from remnants of the ancient riverbeds: the Mullica from the ancient Delaware, and the Great Egg Harbor River from the ancient Schuylkill. Meanwhile, in the West, the Cascade and the Sierra Nevada ranges were being uplifted.

Temperatures gradually fell until the Ice Age occurred, about one million years ago. There were four glacial advances, but at no time did ice reach the Pine Barrens. During the interglacial periods, melting water deposited yellow sand on portions of the Cohansey Formation and laid coarse gravel to

11

the west. During the final advance of ice, the ocean lost water to land ice so that it dropped about 300 feet below its present level, and the coastline moved out approximately ninety miles. The drop was sufficient to expose a land bridge connecting New Jersey, Cape Cod, Nova Scotia and Newfoundland. Many plants are believed to have migrated both north and south along this bridge; some of them still grow in the Pine Barrens. When the last ice melted, the ocean rose to its present level, the Raritan River was diverted eastward into Raritan Bay, and the Pine Barrens took on their current appearance.

The dominant feature of the Pine Barrens is the Cohansey Formation. Water drains quickly through its sandy soil, and nutrients leach away, so lush growth cannot be supported at any distance from the rivers. It does take some time, however, for water to percolate through the sand, and this, together with the formation's great thickness—an average of 75 feet over an area of 1,000 square miles—has created an enormous underground reservoir, or aquifer. The aquifer serves as the region's own headwaters, creating the numerous above-ground streams. Since the area is so large and sand hinders evaporation, the water table is high even during dry seasons, which means that the rivers are generally negotiable. Wells are usually productive even at shallow depths; according to various reports, flows of fifty-five gallons per minute to 500 gallons per minute have been recorded. The brown-colored water is acidic and slightly antiseptic, and this has helped to maintain the aquifer's purity.

Additionally, the Cohansey Formation provides incomes from quarrying. Sand and gravel are excavated everywhere in the Barrens. Building stone, which is sand cemented together with limonite (an iron ore), is quarried near Vineland, and certain minerals are quarried near Lakewood. Atlantic County produces clay; Cumberland County, pure quartz sand. And the mineral ilmenite, a source of titanium, is found in several places.

3

~~~~~~

Human History

In the beginning there were the Lenni Lenape Indians. They lived on both sides of the Delaware River and throughout southern New Jersey. The word Lenape meant "men" or "a people," and Lenni meant "manly" or "original," so the tribal name has been interpreted as both "Manly Men" and "Original People." The Indians canoed the Delaware River and at least one of the Pine Barrens rivers, the Mullica. Their canoes, which they called *moohool*, were either made from elm bark, stretched skins or hollowed logs (called dugouts) that were shaped by repeatedly scorching the wood with hot coals and then scraping away the charcoal.

For food the Lenni Lenape grew pumpkins, corn and beans, gathered blueberries and cranberries, and hunted game and gathered shellfish along the shore. In order to travel more easily across lower New Jersey, they regularly set fires to burn away the underbrush and unwittingly established a curse that has continued to plague the Barrens up to present times. The sight of extensive areas of smoking forests was common to sailors on European ships and led to the naming of Barnegat Bay, which means "burning territory."

The first serious exploration of the area by white men occurred in 1609 when Henry Hudson, working for the Dutch, sailed along the New Jersey coast and up the Hudson River. In

13

1614 Cornelius Mey and Cornelius Hendricksen traveled up the Delaware. Soon Dutch settlers were established along the New Jersey coast and in the Raritan Valley. They were followed by the Swedish, who settled mainly around Delaware Bay but also along the Mullica River. Fishing, trading and, eventually, shipbuilding were the chief occupations. The Dutch maintained control through several decades. England's growing interest in trade, however, led to war between England and Holland, and in 1664 the British occupied New Jersey and New York. Settlers now began arriving from England. Some people, like the Quakers who moved to Burlington County, were fleeing from persecution.

Most of the settlements in south Jersey were located along the coast, the rivers and Delaware Bay. Farmers who tried to grow such traditional crops as corn and vegetables inland from the coast soon learned of the difficulties imposed by the acid, leached-out sand. Records show this area being referred to as the "Barrens" or the "Pines" by 1690. The only people taking an interest in it were a growing number of woodcutters.

Woodcutting

In the seventeenth century, wood was the only construction material available in New Jersey for homes, work places and sailing vessels. Not much time elapsed before settlers, following Indian trails through the Pine Barrens, discovered the fine stands of cedars and pines and the many streams. When dammed, the streams furnished power for sawmills.

Pitch pine, which is soft but light and durable, was made into sills, beams, door and window frames and flooring. Being resistant to decay, it was also used to build ships and to make ship pumps, buckets and waterwheels. Because pine knots have an abundance of resin, pine splints were thrust into holders and lit to serve as torches. The trees themselves were tapped for sap, which was distilled to make turpentine. Pitch tar from waste wood was used as axle grease and medicine. Pine was also smoldered to make charcoal. Cedar is nonresinous and extremely durable, especially when in contact with the ground. It was used extensively for vats, tubs and other woodenware, shingles, interior walls, ship parts and fence posts.

By the beginning of the eighteenth century, the woodcutting industry was well developed, and it progressed to such a degree that in 1749 Benjamin Franklin argued for the adoption of conservation practices, with no apparent effect.

Besides the woodcutters, there were Irish, Scots and English who filtered through the Pine Barrens for their own reasons. England's control had become harsh. It restricted trade in the colonies, particularly in iron and wood, and halted all trade with the West Indies. Conveniently located between the commercial centers in Philadelphia and New York, the murky depths of the Barrens proved ideal for hiding smuggled shipments of goods and transporting them to Philadelphia over sand roads following the Indian trails. As tension rose, smuggling gave way to blatant privateering. Captured British vessels were unloaded at southern New Jersey harbors and their cargoes carried into the forest for distribution.

During the Revolution, and following it, some individuals looked to the Pine Barrens for refuge. After Washington's victory at Trenton, the woods were a haven for Hessian soldiers who deserted the British army. At the end of the war, the Pines became a refuge for Tories fleeing retaliation and for banished Quakers who had violated their code by fighting in the army. These peripheral elements of society had a hard life, and poverty was widespread. Some of them found work cutting wood and making charcoal. Others were able to get by because of growth in the bog-iron and glassmaking industries and later developments in paper manufacturing and agriculture.

Iron Mining

The discovery of bog iron in the Pine Barrens led to a degree of prosperity for some that was previously unknown in the region.

Bog iron is the result of the chemical action of acidic water on an underground layer of iron ore, and it is formed in the following way. Incomplete decomposition of organic material causes groundwater to become acidic. Filtering through sand, the water reaches the layer of greensand marl deposited by the ocean during the formation of southern New Jersey. In the Pine Barrens, the marl lies several hundred feet below the surface, but to the west, it is shallower and even exposed in some places. Greensand contains glauconite, a mineral composed of silicon, potassium and iron. The acidic water dissolves the iron, which diffuses through the underground water and into the rivers. At the surface of the rivers, it is oxidized and sometimes forms a film similar to an oil slick. Some of the iron drifts into still ponds, where the sun, warming the shallow water, drives off the dissolved oxygen, and iron oxide precipitates. It combines with sand and gravel and forms a hard, rocky ore called limonite. Formation of limonite takes place at such a rate that an exhausted ore bed may replenish itself in twenty years. There is a good example of a bed on the Mullica River upstream from Constable Bridge. Limonite can also be seen along the banks of the Manasquan River.

A furnace is required to extract the iron from the ore, and a forge is needed to refine and shape it into the desired form. The furnaces in the Pine Barrens used charcoal and seashells to reduce the ore and waterpower to drive the air bellows. The forges used charcoal for fuel and waterpower to drive the hammers that pounded the pig iron into wrought iron. Thus, not only ore but also wood and running water were essential to the success of the iron industry.

16

The first iron was discovered in Monmouth County in 1675, but mining did not become important until the discovery of rich deposits in the heart of the Pine Barrens and until a demand for iron was created by the French and Indian Wars, the Revolution and the War of 1812. During the wars, iron-works produced cannon and cannonballs, but in between and afterward they manufactured nails, pots, stoves, fences, office furniture, household decorations and many other items. As demand increased, furnaces and forges sprang up throughout the Pine Barrens. Entrepreneurs established themselves, expanded and traded. They lived luxuriously and created a feudal society in the villages; but they worked hard, and their eventual failures resulted from inherent inefficiencies and, perhaps, greed rather than corruption. Workers, though laboring long hours, appeared to be satisfied with the prospect of stable employment. The only signs of restiveness were unscheduled vacations to the coast and the truancy of those who indulged at a nearby tavern.

Many of the ironworks were located on rivers that we canoe today: Atsion, on the Mullica River; Hampton Furnace, Lower Forge and Batsto, on the Batsto River; Speedwell, on the Wading River; Martha Furnace, on the Oswego River; Dover Forge, on Cedar Creek; Mary Ann Furnace, on Mount Misery Brook; and Weymouth, on the Great Egg Harbor River. Martha and Batsto were two of the largest villages. At one time, Martha boasted 400 people and fifty houses, and 800 people lived at Batsto. The War of 1812 gave a final boost to growth, and mining occurred with such fervor that soon after the war the bogs ran short, and iron had to be imported from northern New Jersey and Staten Island. The period from 1812 to 1840 was the high point of the industry; thereafter, it fell to ruins. By 1868 the last furnace had been shut down.

The downfall of the iron industry in the Pines is usually attributed to the rise of the iron industry in Pennsylvania, where coal and a better grade of ore were discovered. Some historians, however, believe that New Jersey iron was doomed with or without Pennsylvania. One of the factors was fire. Most, if not all, of the Jersey ironworks burned down at least once. Enormous amounts of money were spent rebuilding furnaces and villages, and during these times no iron was produced.

A second factor concerned the production of charcoal, which took much time and labor. The trees were cut and the wood was hauled, usually by oxen, to a charcoal burning site, where it was arranged around a chimney in a pile 10 to 20 feet high. The pile (or "pit") was covered with sand, clumps of vegetation and peat gathered from the swamps. It was then allowed to smolder for ten to fourteen days under the supervision of a charcoal tender, called a collier. After the fire was smothered with sand, the charcoal had to be allowed to cool or the wagon carrying it away would catch fire, and this happened occasionally. Finally, the charcoal reached the furnace.

Moreover, an extraordinary number of trees were harvested. Each furnace required at least 30 square miles of forest, harvested on a twenty-year cycle, and only pine was cut for charcoal because other trees produced an inferior grade. The furnace at Batsto used up about 90 square miles of woods. To compound the problem, the woodcutting and charcoal industries began to supply other markets. During the 1840s eight wagons pulled by mule team carried charcoal daily from Weymouth to Philadelphia. At about the same time, fifteen to twenty charcoal-bearing ships sailed regularly between south Jersey and New York City. The misgivings of Benjamin Franklin returned to haunt the ironworks, for they failed at least partially through exhaustion of their timber resources.

The villages, through fire, vandalism and the insecure foundation provided by sand, gradually disappeared, and no trace is left of most of them. All that remains of Martha, for instance, is rubble buried underground. There are a few restored houses at Atsion. Most of the relics salvaged in the Pines have been moved to Batsto, where the village is being restored by the state.

Glassmaking

With its limitless quantity of good sand, southern New Jersey was a natural site for a glassmaking industry. And there was a demand for glass in the early 1700s that England could not satisfy. The first successful glassworks in the United States was established in 1739, south of the Pine Barrens in Salem County, by Caspar Wistar, who brought four glass craftsmen from Germany. They produced primarily bottles and window glass but also created artistic pieces that became known as Wistarberg glass. Unfortunately, the factory closed during the Revolution, partly because Caspar's son Richard, the manager, considered himself a Tory in alien land and did not want to contribute to the American cause.

At about this time the Stanger family, whose sons worked for Wistar, established the Olive Glass Works at what is now Glassboro. The factory expanded and combined with other operations to make Glassboro the major center of New Jersey glass. Later it merged with the Owens Bottle Company and eventually became part of the Libbey-Owens-Ford Company. It produced most of the surviving pieces of what is known as South Jersey glass. Among other items, the factory made a spirits bottle in the shape of a log cabin, following the design of Philadelphia liquor dealer Edmund Booz. It became known as the Booz bottle, so its contents were called booze. The name lives on in our vocabulary long after the container has disappeared.

The Wheaton Glass Factory in Millville is still active. Started in the later 1800s, it produces blood plasma bottles nowadays. Other glassworks were not as fortunate. The Coffin factory in

19

Hammonton, built in 1817, acquired fame for producing unusual whiskey flasks. During the latter days of the bog-iron industry, glass was made at Batsto. At Crowleytown, just below Batsto, a glass factory produced the first Mason jar, designed by John L. Mason of Vineland, in 1858. The Lebanon Glass House manufactured bottles and fancy walking sticks, and later converted to window glass. All of these glassworks were forced to close during the late 1860s for lack of wood to fuel the furnaces. Fires were common as well; the glassworks at Batsto was put out of commission by fire at least four times during its short existence. Not long after the various factories closed down, their buildings were destroyed by more fires.

Papermaking

For a time there was a small paper industry in the Pine Barrens. A papermill was built at Atsion, but it failed only a few years later in the depression of 1854. A mill at Harrisville was more successful. Replacing an iron forge that had fallen on hard times, the paper factory was established there in 1832. The main building was an enormous structure two and a half stories high and several hundred feet long. The raw material for the paper was salt grass from the tidewater marshes of the Mullica River. To make the paper, the grass was steamed to remove salt and other soluble residues. It was then macerated into a pulp and rolled into sheets. The resulting product was a very strong wrapping paper. A writing paper was also produced, but it was not popular because it had a yellowish tinge from the iron in the water used in the manufacturing process. The Harrisville factory and village flourished to the extent that ornamental gas street lamps illuminated the main thoroughfare and were famous throughout the Pine Barrens. But the mill ceased operation in 1889 because of competition, depressions and the owner's inability to route a rail line through the town. In 1914 the buildings were destroyed by fire. Soon after, the street lamps and all other pieces of metal were removed by junkmen, and vandals finished off the rest. Today, a crumbling wall covered with bushes is all that remains of Harrisville.

A cotton mill was built at Pleasant Mills in 1822. After a fire in 1855 (there had been a previous one in 1834), it was abandoned and then rebuilt as a paper mill that used Jersey salt grass. The paper mill prospered despite two more fires but was finally closed in 1915 because of transportation difficulties and fuel shortages brought on by World War I. Recently, it was rebuilt again to operate as a summer playhouse.

Agriculture

Commercial farming in the Pine Barrens is limited to crops that thrive on sandy, acid soil—generally, acidic fruits. Among them, the cranberry reigns. It was valued by the Indians for food and ritual. To protect it, the New Jersey legislature in 1789 passed an act prohibiting the picking of cranberries on public land between June 1 and October 10. Cranberry cultivation began in 1840 in Burlington County, which today is the leading grower in the state. In 1889 the fruit's culinary possibilities were introduced to England by a New Jersey citizen, Andrew Rider, who founded Rider College in Trenton. Nowadays the production of cranberries in New Jersey is exceeded only by that in Wisconsin and Massachusetts. In 1988, according to the New Jersey Department of Agricultural Statistics, cranberries were grown on 33,000 acres, which produced a record crop of 370,000 barrels.

Cranberries are grown in bogs—depressed fields that are flooded by controlling the flow of streams. Flooding takes place in the fall at harvest time and in the winter as protection from frost. During harvesting, the berries are pulled from the plants by one-horsepower machines that are rolled manually over the

21

submersed fields. Floating to the surface of the water, the scarlet berries are blown by the wind to the shore, where pickers gather them and conveyors load them onto trucks. Harvesting takes place in October; this colorful sight may be seen wherever a highway passes cranberry bogs, such as on Route 563 south of Chatsworth.

At the packing plant, the cranberries are automatically washed and separated from accompanying twigs, leaves and soil. Then they are conveyed to the top of a scaffold and allowed to bounce down a series of shelves. According to their bounce—soft, medium or hard—they land in different bins, which determines their grade for the market. After a final inspection, they are packed and shipped.

Blueberries are also natural to the Pine Barrens and began to be cultivated about fifteen years after cranberries. In 1988, 7,700 acres of blueberry land, mostly in Atlantic and Burlington counties, produced 22 million pounds of fruit, which increased some 7 million pounds the following year. Cultivated blueberries are bred not so much for flavor as for size and ease in harvesting by machine. The blueberry-picking machine is taller than the bushes and has a cab mounted above, where the driver sits. The legs of the machine are as far apart as the spacing between rows, and each leg has what city dwellers identify as subway turnstiles. In operation the machine straddles the row, and as it moves along, the tines of the "turnstiles" shake the bushes vigorously and flick off the ripe berries, which fall into a receptacle.

Apples, too, are a major crop. They are picked by hand. The Pine Barrens produce two early varieties: a form of Delicious and Stayman-Winesap.

The city of Vineland was founded by Charles Landis, who hoped to establish a grape industry there. It was not successful. But one grower, a Methodist dentist named Thomas Welch, learned how to apply the results of Pasteur's experiments to the bottling of grape juice so that it might serve as a substitute for wine at religious services, wine being thought improper by church leaders. Welch and his son founded the company that is still in business. It has since moved to New York. A more permanent Jersey grape business was begun in 1859 in Egg Harbor City when Louis Renault established a vineyard and began to produce champagne. The business still operates today.

The Wharton Tract and Public Lands

The Pine Barrens, perhaps because of their inhospitable aspect, have always attracted speculators and promoters eager to claim the area's resources, and financier Joseph Wharton was no exception. Cognizant of the extensive underground reservoir, Wharton, a Philadelphian, set out to accumulate Pine Barrens acreage with the purpose of selling the water rights to his hometown. Beginning in 1876, he bought many tracts on which sawmills, gristmills, ironworks, glassworks, and paper-mills had failed, until he owned 100,000 acres. In some properties, such as Batsto, he took an active interest, restoring buildings and continuing whatever could be done to earn an income. He also dabbled in cattle and sugar beets. His main objective, however—that of becoming a water merchant—was thwarted when the New Jersey legislature learned of his intentions and passed an act forbidding the export of water.

After Wharton's death in 1909, his land, which had become known collectively as the Wharton Tract, was offered for sale to the state. The state was interested in the tract's potential as a watershed, but Burlington, Atlantic and Camden counties together with nine townships stood to lose the taxes the land was providing and were opposed to the sale. Negotiations dragged on for years. Finally, in 1954 the deal was consummated in two stages, and the Wharton Tract became a state forest.

Since then, public interest has spurred the state's acquisition of additional land, much of it close to the Wharton Tract. The largest areas are Lebanon State Forest, Penn State Forest, Bass River State Forest and Belleplain State Forest. Smaller parcels lie on Cedar Creek, the Manasquan River and the Great Egg Harbor River. The state Division of Fish, Game and Shellfisheries controls Colliers Mills, and the state has a quail farm on the Toms River. A public group, the Friends of the Rancocas, maintains land bordering Rancocas Creek as a wildlife sanctuary. All told, these properties constitute about 15 percent of the land in the Pine Barrens.

The Pineys

When most of the industrial enterprises failed in the second half of the nineteenth century, the inhabitants of the Pines found themselves destitute. Many descendants of the settlers who had found advantage in the Barrens—Indians, Dutch and Swedish woodcutters, English smugglers, Quakers and Hessian soldiers—moved away. Those who remained came to terms with the woods and were able to earn a subsistence by bending with the seasons. In the spring they gathered sphagnum moss to sell to florists and horticulturists. In the summer they picked blueberries; in the fall, cranberries. In the winter they cut cordwood and, until World War II, made charcoal. For winter holidays they gathered pine cones and branches of laurel, holly, cedar and pine. Today, the local people (who may not appreciate being called "pineys") live along county roads or in the woods; their story was told by John McPhee in his book *The Pine Barrens*.

Two of the better known legends among the pineys concern James Still, the "Black Doctor" of the Pines, and the Jersey Devil. James Still was a black man who lived during the 1800s and taught himself medicine by reading books and learning

24

herb lore from Indians. He had a difficult time because of his color; nevertheless, he traveled through the woods practicing a trade that utilized his unique background, and eventually he earned a following that revered him throughout his life.

The Jersey Devil, a legendary monster, is claimed to be real by some residents and has been observed by honest and hard-working men. The most popular account of its origin is that it was born to a Mrs. Leeds, who, having already had twelve children, exclaimed before its birth: "I don't want no baby. I hope the next one's a devil." Sure enough, the thirteenth baby was a monstrosity, and it has plagued the land ever since. The Jersey Devil's appearance is said to foretell impending disasters; sightings have been reported before local shipwrecks and wars as far back as the Revolution.

The Present and Future

One of the long-standing problems in the Pine Barrens has been an uncertainty of land ownership, resulting largely from the hodgepodge of failed enterprises. Families have lived for generations on land they believe to be theirs; actually, it may belong to the descendants of earlier owners who never bothered to live there. Occasionally, land was traded by verbal agreement. Some people have never paid taxes because of confusion over who owns what, and even today unscrupulous dealers sell land having no clear title.

Until recently, none of this seemed to matter much. The local people still cut cordwood and gather plants for a living. Fires still occur—in a twenty-to-twenty-five-year cycle in most places and an eight-to-ten-year cycle in others—but the forest has adapted and manages to survive the equilibrium. To anyone who does not look closely, much of the Pines appears to be virgin land.

The times, however, are changing. There is a new threat,

not from extraction of natural resources but from residential development. The increasing population growth in northern New Jersey and metropolitan Philadelphia has caused developers to expand into the Pine Barrens. Vast mobile home communities are being established. As a ploy to obtain the necessary zoning changes from a township, some developers arranged to market their developments as "adult communities," which means no children. The municipality benefited from increased taxes on new structures without having to provide the most expensive service, namely, schooling.

Leaving aside the discordant design of these communities, where no attempt is made to blend them into their surroundings, these developments create four problems. First, they increase land values and cause farm taxes to rise considerably despite New Jersey's Farmland Assessment Act. To cite an example, not far from Cedar Creek is an 8,000-unit mobile-home community that caused land values and tax assessments to multiply unrealistically for any purpose other than building more mobile-home communities. As a result, the cranberry grower at Double Trouble was forced out of business. The second problem is a loss of recreational land in an area where recreational demand is growing rapidly. The third is the effect of probable fires on densely populated communities situated in a region having a long history of fires. And the fourth is the effect of developments' septic tanks on the quality of the underground reservoir.

Initial steps to protect the Pinelands from incompatible development and uses were taken in the early 1960s when a huge jetport was proposed to be built in the dwarf or pygmy pine forest. Environmental organizations formed FOCUS (Federation of Conservationists, United Societies, Inc.), and were able to defeat the proposal by arousing public opinion against it. Following this success, the group organized the Pinelands Advisory Committee to seek a long-term solution for preservation

26

and protection of the Pine Barrens. On the recommendation of the Committee, the legislature created the Pinelands Environmental Council and commissioned it to devise a master plan for the Pines. The council was plagued with political scandals from the start, and its completed plan was labeled "a developer's dream." Since the council was advisory only and had no real power over development, it was completely ineffective. Governor Brendan T. Byrne appointed a Pinelands Review Committee to study the region and recommend effective means to protect it. As a result of the Committee's deliberations, Congress designated the Pinelands as the nation's first National Reserve in 1978. In June, 1979, New Jersey passed the Pinelands Protection Act and the newly formed Pinelands Commission was given authority over all development within a one-million-acre region. The Comprehensive Management Plan (CMP) for the New Jersey Pinelands, passed in January, 1981, is a unique, regional framework for local decisions, written in a cooperative effort by public, scientific and economic experts and the fifteen-member Pinelands Commission.

The goals of the plan were to 1) preserve essential areas through federal, state and local funding and acquisition, and 2) develop methods of safeguarding the Pinelands while recognizing the tradition of private ownership. As a rough guide, the Pinelands were divided into two regions: the "Pinelands Preservation Area," an inner core with severe regulations intended to preserve the wilderness character of the Pine Barrens; and the surrounding "Pinelands Protection Area," where regulations are more relaxed. The preservation area includes the Wharton Tract and the pine plains, or pygmy forest, in Ocean and Burlington counties. The Pinelands Protection Act requires that local zoning ordinances and master plans be brought into conformity with the CMP.

Much has happened to preserve the Pinelands. Part of the

Mullica River is now included in the New Jersey Wild and Scenic River System. The state has acquired a considerable amount of land along rivers. The uppermost section of the Great Egg Harbor River is now a wildlife management area, and the best part of Cedar Creek is a state park. Atlantic County is developing a linear park system, which includes the lower end of the Great Egg Harbor River. Part of the south branch of the Metedeconk River is in the Lake Shenandoah County Park and Field Sports Complex. And Winding River Park has saved a portion of the Toms River from development.

Nevertheless, confidence in the ability to preserve the Pinelands has eroded. There are constant efforts to weaken the Pinelands Protection Act by lawsuits, amendments, appointment of Pinelands Commission members who prefer development to preservation and the most narrow interpretation possible of the various laws (for example, that the New Jersey Natural Areas System was intended only to protect small areas primarily for scientific study, rather than larger areas such as the Pine Barrens). The Pinelands Commission has the unenviable task of placating private; local and state opposition. Municipalities were supposed to have brought their ordinances into compliance with the CMP by January 1982, but as of this writing they have not yet done so. Since 1981, 24,000 new houses have been built in the Pinelands Protection Area. The conflict between development and the environment in the protection area still rages, and the environment, which is poorly funded and supported by fragmented organizations, is getting the worst of it. Even within the Pinelands Preservation Area, the master plan has been blocked by a conflict between environmental groups and users of off-road vehicles.

As events now stand, two major efforts are bolstering environmental interests. In reaction to the continuing degradation of the Pinelands and to give themselves more clout, local environmental groups recently formed the Pinelands Preservation Alliance to revive grass-roots efforts to preserve the Pinelands, to monitor the activities of the Pinelands Commission and to hire a full-time professional person to run the organization. To address the specific problem of how the preservation area is used, the New Jersey chapter of the Sierra Club, with support from many other local and interested groups, submitted a proposal in 1984 to set aside the four major rivers in the Wharton Tract, the wilderness area between them, the Batona hiking trail and the pygmy forest as regions allowing only activities compatible with a wilderness setting. These regions would be open to most recreational uses but closed to most off-road vehicles, which would be permitted only for administrative purposes. So far, however, the proposal is only being studied.

What can individuals who wish to preserve the rivers and other wilderness areas in the Pine Barrens do? They can, of course, support the efforts of local environmental groups and remain current on activities concerning the Pine Barrens. Another suggestion is to write the New Jersey Pinelands Commission, P.O. Box 7, New Lisbon, NJ 08064, or call (609) 894-9342. The Pinelands Commission offers a periodic publication, "The Pinelander," free of charge to interested persons.

4

~~~~~~

Beer Cans and Bleach Bottles

The second edition of *Webster's International Dictionary* defines the word pollute as follows: "to make or render impure or unclean, ceremonially, physically, or morally; to impair or destroy the purity or sanctity of; to defile; desecrate; profane; corrupt; befoul." Therefore, the material in this chapter logically belongs in the preceding chapter because pollution is a part of human history. I isolate the subject of pollution to emphasize those activities that, because of recent publicity or increased abuse, are regarded by most people as antisocial—air pollution, water pollution, littering and vandalism.

Apparently, there is no air pollution in the Pine Barrens, although there is around the perimeter. Just try to locate stars near the horizon on a clear night. Water pollution does exist in the rivers near concentrated residential areas. The state is becoming aware of it and will, we hope, attend to it because of the government's stake in maintaining the purity of the aquifer. Both littering and vandalism are present in the Pines. We, as canoeists, should be particularly aware of these two evils.

Littering

The Pine Barrens is touched by litter everywhere. In terms of mass, most of it is deposited by people wishing to rid their households of trash. Tires, oil drums, plastic in all forms, aluminum cans and paper are found along the back roads and sometimes on riverbanks and in the water. For sheer volume, however, those coming to the Pines for sports and recreation win the litterbug award. This group includes canoeists, hunters and people looking for a good time. Locals or near-locals have favorite riverbank hangouts: Parking areas on the Toms River at Whitesville and on the Rancocas at Browns Mills are two examples. Many canoeists and campers use the rivers for partying.

What can be done about litter? The best solution is to prevent it, but this does not seem practical. One would have to set up roadblocks on every road leading into the Pine Barrens and hand out free trashbags, and even that might not succeed. The alternative is to clean it up. At the present time some rivers are maintained by individuals, usually associated with canoe rental agencies, and by the South Jersey Canoe Club. In locations where the state is developing the river for recreational use, such as at Cedar Creek, pressure is being exerted to persuade canoe rental agencies to remove litter, much of it left by their customers.

Another possibility is to conduct local cleanup parties. Such an operation was carried out in 1969 on Rancocas Creek, between Browns Mills and New Lisbon. It was sponsored by the New York Chapter of the Appalachian Mountain Club, and Boy Scouts were recruited from Browns Mills. Until recently, that section of the Rancocas remained reasonably clean, but it has become littered again.

Besides the common form of littering encountered in the Pines and elsewhere, there is another type found here: the littering of wood debris. A contractor or landowner may clear a tract of land and dump the logs, branches and undergrowth into a nearby river because that is cheaper than hauling it away. The practice is illegal under Section 10 of the Rivers and

31

Harbors Act of 1899, which prohibits dredging, filling or obstructing navigable waters without a permit from the U.S. Army Corps of Engineers. Although the Corps has been accused of issuing permits without properly determining the impact of a project on the environment, it may not issue a permit after the fact. Anyone who wishes to complain about a river obstruction should write to: U.S. Army Engineer District, Philadelphia; Attention: Operations Division; U.S. Custom House; Second & Chestnut Street; Philadelphia, PA 19106. Results may take awhile because the remoteness of the rivers usually requires an aerial inspection, and if the inspection is made during a time of high water, the obstruction may be partially or completely submerged.

In 1974 I found two severe blockages, both obviously caused by litter from cleared land, on the Great Egg Harbor River and Oyster Creek. I reported the blockages to the Corps of Engineers, who acknowledged my letter but apparently ignored it, because nothing happened. Nevertheless, river obstructions, with the possible exception of a footbridge that requires a single liftover, should be reported to the Corps. Similar complaints by several people may bring a more serious, prompt response.

Vandalism

Vandalism is not always obvious to a canoeist in the Pines. I was only marginally aware of it before preparing this guidebook. But it does occur. For instance, an elderly landowner in the area was plagued by people who used his property without permission and took his boat; now he will not let anyone cross his property, even when they ask permission. Some canoe campers were harassed on a riverbank, accessible by a back road, where they had camped safely on many occasions. Vandals tampered with the floodgates at one cranberry field; the

32

owner of another had to dig a ditch to keep people away. Elsewhere, siding was ripped from a barn for firewood. Another barn was burned down by boys who started a campfire on the floor. There are reports of people throwing torches from moving cars into the woods and of stolen automobiles set on fire.

Within the last few years, the incidence of car damage has increased. Cars have been broken into at the Pleasant Mills take-out from the Mullica River; cars were damaged at the put-in to the Oswego River; tires were damaged at the put-in to Cedar Creek at Lacey Road; a trailer was vandalized at Evans Bridge on the Wading River; and a trailer was stolen in Pemberton. One remedy to protecting a car in Wharton State Forest is to park at the ranger stations, free for anyone with a camping permit. Some private campgrounds (Cedar Creek Campground, for example) offer a shuttle service for a nominal charge.

These examples are not meant to scare visitors away from the Pine Barrens. Such incidents and worse are common throughout the country. One should, however, be aware of the possibility of vandalism and exercise prudence. Also, it is important to understand that the hostility of riverbank landowners is sometimes the result of vandalism to their property, and one should ask permission to use their property whenever possible. In addition, incidents of vandalism should be reported to the nearest authorities.

5

Pine Trees and Pitcher Plants

The characteristics that distinguish one Pine Barrens river from another stem from the interplay between water and plants. A river's current may be moderate or slow. It may flow along a well-defined channel or spread out into a pond. Heavy rainfall may cause it to overflow its banks and flood the adjoining land, where drainage may be good or poor. All these things affect the nature of the plants growing along the banks. Conversely, the flora helps to determine the character of the river. Trees may shade the stream, restrict the passage of a canoe or stand in splendid isolation among fields of grasses. Bushes, brambles, rushes and underwater grasses may hinder passage on water or land. The shapes, textures and colors of the plants, changing continuously from season to season and even from one location to another, offer an infinite variety of patterns.

Whether one would enjoy oneself more in the Pines as a botanist possessing no canoeing skills or as a canoeist with no knowledge of botany is an open question; fortunately, there are enough attractions for both botanists and canoeists. But an excellent argument for pursuing a knowledge of plant life was put forth by Charles Darwin in his *Voyage of the Beagle:*

> I am strongly induced to believe that, as in music, the person who understands every note will, if he also pos-

34

sesses a proper taste, more thoroughly enjoy the whole, so he who examines each part of a fine view, may also thoroughly comprehend the full and combined effect. Hence a traveller should be a botanist, for in all views plants form the chief embellishment.

Common River Plants

One interesting feature of the Pine Barrens is that the region is a meeting place for a small number of plants from the North and a large number from the South. Northern plants migrated to New Jersey during the Ice Age across an ancient land bridge connecting New Jersey with Cape Cod and points north. Southern plants grow here because the Pine Barrens share the same early geologic history with the coastal plain of the South.

According to a present estimate, there are more than 800 species of plants in the Barrens. In 1916 John W. Harshberger listed 548 species according to their periods of flowering and fruiting. Of these, 19 were ferns and mosses, 156 were grass-like plants, 22 were trees, 61 were shrubs and the remaining 290 were flowering herbaceous plants. The few common plants that Harshberger missed were more than balanced out by the enormous number of rare and inconspicuous species that he managed to observe. Actually, a knowledge of even a few of these plants is sufficient to give the canoeist an appreciation for the region he or she is paddling through.

The pitch pine is the most common tree. It grows primarily in dry, sandy upland soil, where it is generally the dominant growth. Even then, it is only of medium size, and scattered, with the space between trees usually filled by a variety of shrubs. To a canoeist, seeing a patch of pine trees is the only sure sign of a dry stopping place.

Another common conifer is the white cedar. In contrast to the pine, it grows along the water's edge in damp soil. Occasionally its forests are so dense that they suffocate other growth. On some rivers it forms a wall of deep green on both sides which is decorated only by a slight, shrubby growth that manages to survive the dim light. The white cedar is the tallest tree I have seen in the Pine Barrens.

People who have trouble distinguishing a pitch pine from a white cedar should note that the leaves of the pine are long and needle shaped and grouped in bunches of three. The leaves of the cedar, on the other hand, are very short, numerous and attached to one another in a branched, flattened spray. Once the trees can be identified by their leaves, additional differences are usually noticed.

The most common deciduous trees are oaks and maples. Oaks are found in upland sites, sometimes as the dominant growth, but near the rivers they are rare. An exception is the willow oak, which occasionally grows along the riverbank. Its leaves are delicate and graceful—long and narrow like a willow's but with sharp, thorny tips. The red maple is everywhere in the swamps. Rooting in waterlogged soil, it has little competition from other trees, except cedar. The leaves are smaller than those of most maples and are toothed, with three pointed lobes.

Additional trees seen now and then are holly, an evergreen with small thorny leaves; swamp magnolia or sweet bay, whose large, oval light green leaves stay green in the south and nearly so in the Pine Barrens; sweet gum, whose leaf has five deep, uniformly pointed lobes diverging from the base; sassafras, with mitten-shaped leaves having one, two or three rounded lobes; and hard gum, which is not related to sweet gum and often goes unnoticed because of its undistinguished, small, smooth oval leaves.

Of the most numerous shrubs, about half are members of the heath family: evergreen laurels, leatherleaf, cranberry, de-

36

ciduous swamp azalea, blueberry and huckleberry. Some grow in swamps, others upland. Many look the same because of their oval, smooth-edged leaves. But the leaves of laurels and azaleas are large, whereas the rest are small. The flowers of the laurels are like cups, the azaleas are like long, flared tubes and most of the other heaths are like tiny urns.

The most prominent large upland bushes growing among the pines are not heaths, however, but several varieties of scrub oak. They have large leaves with rounded lobes. Likewise, the most prominent large bush in the swamps is not a heath but the sweet pepperbush. It can be identified throughout the year by its persistent flower stalks—short stems projecting upward that bear either uniformly distributed remnants of flowers or small, hard fruit resembling white peppercorns. Another common bush along the rivers is inkberry, an evergreen with shiny, dark green leaves and tiny, black berries. Other bushes often seen along the banks are shadbush (juneberry), black alder (winterberry), viburnum, buttonbush and smooth or common alder. Many shrubs are difficult for a beginner to recognize without their flowers—first of all, because of the incredible density of riparian growth and secondly, because of the similarity of leaf shapes. Still, after learning to recognize a bush by its flowers, one often notices features that will distinguish it in flowerless seasons.

Only three varieties of vines are common along the rivers: catbrier, poison ivy and, less often, grape. Catbrier is everywhere in the deciduous swamps, crawling over bushes and down into the water or hanging like great broad sheets from trees. It even prohibits passage by foot along dry ground. Hanging over the rivers, it can be spectacular from a distance but a real nuisance in no time because its tough stems may entangle canoes or their passengers and its thorns inflict wounds and tear shirts. River-clearing parties spend an appre-

37

ciable portion of time trimming brier. Poison ivy, as most people know, has its own way of commanding respect; a detailed description appears later in this chapter. Any vine that is neither brier nor poison ivy is most likely grape and can be identified by its very large, sharp-lobed leaves. Virginia creeper has been reported in the Pine Barrens. I may have overlooked it, but I did not see any along the rivers. It can be recognized by five leaflets gathered together at the same point on the leaf stalk.

Wherever the current of the rivers slows down, grass-like plants appear, sometimes growing thinly on the banks and mixed with shrubs, and elsewhere forming vast fields in standing water. They often group closely in hummocks—bunches 2 to 4 feet across. The flat-bladed sedges and grasses grow together and are difficult to distinguish. Round and slender rushes, which are red at water level but blend quickly to green toward the tip, are found farther out in the water, closer to the main current. On some rivers, often where there are cedar trees, beds of pipewort grow in the middle of the stream, completely submersed, with long, flat-bladed leaves trailing gracefully in the current. It may grow so densely that it resembles a large, green boulder on the river bottom. Another subaqueous plant found in moving water is the water club rush, with long, hairlike leaves.

The flowers of the Pine Barrens are spectacular but ephemeral, and the plants that produce most of them are otherwise little noticed. The leaves of some water plants are more persistent: blue flag iris, with its tall, linear leaves; water lilies; and duckweed, which forms a mat of tiny green discs that look like clover leaves on the surface of the water. Several plants with heart-shaped to arrow-shaped leaves grow in the rivers. Among them are arrowhead, with delicate leaves and white flowers; pickerel weed, with purple flowers; and green arrow arum, with a spathe flower. Swamp loosestrife, or water willow, grows in water and is useful in the evolution of a bog. It is a coarse-looking plant with a tall stalk and leaves arranged on the stalk in circles of three. In boggy places one can fortuitously spot beds of tiny sundews, with sticky droplets at the ends of the stems. Sometimes when the water level is low in the fall, one can find large patches of sundews on exposed mud flats. Close to the rivers and more conspicuous are the pitcher plants. Their water-holding receptacles are arranged in a rosette pattern, and their leaves, although green in the shade, turn red in bright sunlight.

Among the nonflowering plants, mosses and ferns are common. Mosses grow on damp ground, particularly around the base of trees, and on tree trunks. Ferns may be found on damp, shaded ground and also on high, arid land, where they are mixed with low heaths, scrub oaks and pines.

Seasonal Changes

In the early spring, toward the end of March, the first flowers begin to appear. Oval catkins, faintly resembling tiny pine cones, open up on common alders growing along the riverbanks. A most charming sight are little urn-shaped flowers of leatherleaf, which dangle in a row from the end of their stalk at the water's edge in marshy areas. The brownish tinge and coarse texture of evergreen leaves account for the plant's name. At about the same time, the maple flowers are out, a spray of bright crimson. The colors of the early flowers balance well against the evergreens in these first days. On the lower end of the Batsto River, for example, one panoramic view takes in green pine needles, darker green cedars, the dark blue-green, waxy leaves of inkberry, the scurfy leaves and greenish white flowers of leatherleaf, straw-colored grasses, red maple flowers, deep purple-red cranberry leaves and the bright red leaves of pitcher plants.

39

The red maple flowers are replaced by red-winged fruit around the middle of April; it colors the streams so much that it gives them an autumnal aspect. The straw remnants of the previous year's grasses are slowly replaced by emerald fields of new growth. Gradually, the maple leaves unfold. The leaves of pickerel weed appear in or along the edge of the water, which is usually at a high level at this time of year. In early May, the light green leaves of sweet pepperbush contrast brightly with dormant branches of other shrubs. Juneberry bushes distinguish themselves by their white flowers with five petals and many red-tipped stamens. The slender, tubular white flowers of swamp azalea appear. High-bush blueberries bloom along the banks, bearing the urn-shaped flowers that are typical of many plants in the heath family. Thorny catbrier shows its small flowers. Gray birch trees display drooping catkins. The fiddleheads of ferns sprout up and gradually unfold. White violets blossom on the banks. In the still waters alongside the streams and in the lakes, golden club sends up its white, gold-tipped stalks. The flowers of pitcher plants, ready to open, look like deep purple-red globes dropping from their stalks. On the higher dry banks, the low and creeping sand myrtle is in bloom, displaying small, white flowers with dark red stamens. Sometimes one can see false heather in flower at the same time—a pale, normally inconspicuous creeping shrub with dense, needlelike leaves, which displays a brilliant assembly of yellow flowers at this season.

By June all leaves are out. Blue-colored irises and pickerel weed flowers are in bloom, projecting from the water. White and yellow water lilies are quite splendid, dotting the surface with luxurious blooms. Small, white viburnum flowers cluster in large groups with flat-topped crowns. Big swamp magnolia flowers begin to appear. The remaining heath shrubs are in bloom: the white, cup-shaped flowers of mountain laurel; the smaller pink flowers of sheep laurel; the tiny, pink flowers of cranberry; and the urn-shaped flowers of other species. Several large heaths with blossoms similar to the high-bush blueberry's can be seen along the water's edge. The flowers of the staggerbush are half again as large, those of the dangleberry more globular and those of the fetterbush narrower.

The flowers of the holly family also appear, but they are small and grouped in clusters close to the leaves. The most common is inkberry, with its dark evergreen leaves, but winterberry, with similar flowers, can also be seen. Later in June and in the month of July, small, irregular, pink pogonia orchids are prevalent along the shores and in boggy areas. Ripening high-bush blueberries, with their tiny crowns and whitish blooms, should not be confused with the darker, shiny berries of other bushes, which are not good to eat.

July and August are the most fragrant months of the year because then the multitude of white sweet pepperbush flowers springs forth along short vertical stalks. The dense, globular heads of buttonbush appear now and can be seen into September. Occasionally one may recognize meadow beauties, striking purple flowers with four petals and yellow stamens, in open, grassy fields near water.

In September and October, purple asters appear on the drier riverbanks. Grasses, sedges and rushes also begin to flower now and through the fall. (Their flowers require a special study.) In October the long stalks of underwater pipewort, with small dark nodules at their tips, project from the riverbeds and bend downstream with the leaves.

September is more properly the beginning of the major fruiting season for swamp plants and the color changes that signal dormancy. Brier berries are green and gradually turning black. Mushrooms are out, gracefully protruding from sand, logs, roots of overturned trees and beds of moss. Sweet pep-

41

perbush displays its small, round capsules. Identical bright red berries appear on the female holly trees and their cousin, winterberry; the other cousin, inkberry, has black berries. Ferns in the dry uplands have turned brown.

In October cranberries are ripe and succulent and invigorating on frosty days if one is prepared for their tart flavor. Sweet pepperbush leaves are yellow, maple leaves red, brier a dark purple, sweet gum leaves a bright purple, oak leaves a dingy yellow-brown and low heath shrubs crimson. Viburnum is conspicuous because of its reddish brown leaves and flat clusters of oval berries, which are pink at first but gradually turn deep blue. October is a month of both pastel colors and bright contrasts, especially among bushes on high ground. In some places one sees primarily yellow and brownish red ferns and scrub oaks, and in others the brilliant green of sheep laurel against the crimson of the heaths. In the usual low water of early fall, the arrow arum can be seen, with its bulbous stalk drooping on the muddy banks.

By the middle of November, most of the deciduous leaves are on the ground or floating on the water, where they may collect in dense layers behind patches of debris. The red berries of winterberry, still hanging from otherwise denuded branches, contrast with the gray-brown of dormant bushes or, more rarely, the green of mountain laurel. The underwater plants are still green. Now and through the winter, the evergreen plants, formerly little noticed, stand out: dark inkberry; shiny-leafed mountain laurel; lighter dull-leafed sheep laurel; rusty-leafed leatherleaf; creeping, dark cranberry; holly; pines and cedars. Swamp magnolias still display their large, light green leaves. The persistent fruit of sweet pepperbush will last well into the next season. Then maples may be located by their new growth of red twigs and buds grow symmetrically from older branches. And one may see large, fat, multi-tinted buds at the tips of swamp azalea branches.

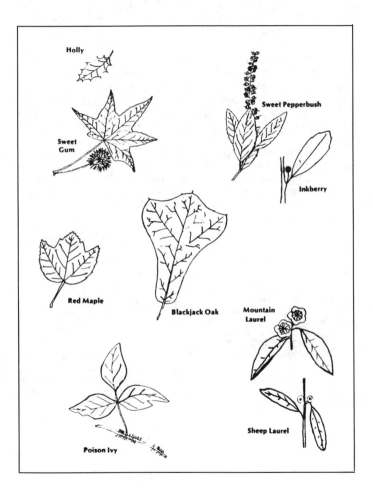

Holly

Sweet Pepperbush

Sweet Gum

Inkberry

Red Maple

Blackjack Oak

Mountain Laurel

Poison Ivy

Sheep Laurel

Plant Communities

The many ecological niches of Pine Barrens vegetation are grouped in three broad categories: treeless marshes, where land is flooded throughout the year, or almost so; lowlands, where there is flooding part of the year or where the ground-water is high enough to affect vegetation; and uplands, where the water table is low and drainage through porous sand is swift.

The marshes comprise ponds, savannas and bush communities. Pond vegetation occurs wherever the river current is sufficiently slow—still water to the side of a main channel, backed up into a pool or at the entrance and borders of a lake. The easily recognized pond plants are white and yellow water lilies, blue flag iris, pickerel weed, golden club and various grasses. All the rivers have such vegetation somewhere in their course. A savanna in the Pine Barrens definition of the word is a flooded area of grasses. The Mullica, Batsto and Wading rivers have savannas. In some places, as on the Mullica River above Atsion, there are treeless fields not of grasses but of bushes, chiefly leatherleaf. These are called bush communities or spongs (pronounced "spungs"). The word is probably derived from "spongy," which is as descriptive a term as one could apply to these areas.

The lowlands comprise bogs, swamps and pine transition communities. The difference between a bog and a swamp is not always well defined; the terms are often used interchangeably. In this book, a bog is an area of poor drainage; a place where there are floating mats of sphagnum moss; or a spot where cedar trees are at their ultimate growth. A swamp is an area of better drainage where a primarily deciduous forest grows.

A bog is likely to form in an area of low, stagnant water. Because there is poor water circulation, dissolved oxygen is quickly used up and vegetative matter decomposes only partially. Eventually it turns into peat. The peat retains nutritive components and alkaline elements, so the water turns acidic. This restricts most growth except that of sphagnum moss. Moss flourishes and forms mats on the water, supported by such plants as swamp loosestrife. After a continuous period of growth and decay, during which peat sinks to the bottom and gradually makes the water more shallow, the mats of sphagnum moss become strong enough to support plants, shrubs and eventually cedar trees, which grow quickly and establish their dominance. In very dense cedar bogs, such as those on the Oswego River, little else that requires light survives. But carnivorous pitcher plants and sundews grow because they get the nutrients they need from insects. In less-dense growths of cedar, there may be some heaths and scattered pines.

Swamps produce less peat than bogs and have more fertile soil. With the superior soil and better drainage, deciduous trees do well. Red maples are dominant, but one will see swamp magnolias, sweet gums, black gums and sassafras. Sweet pepperbush is the most prevalent shrub. Various heaths are also common. Swamps constitute most of the lowlands in the Pine Barrens and appear along all the rivers.

Pine transition communities bridge the gap between wet bogs and swamps and well-drained uplands. They occur on the Mullica, Batsto, Wading and Toms rivers, among others. There, scattered pitch pines are the only trees, and shrubs are well represented. In the poorly drained sections of the transition communities, leatherleaf is the most common bush. In the better-drained sections, sheep laurel is common and is the key plant for identifying this environment.

The uplands comprise several communities in which combinations of pines and oaks predominate. In the most common one, pitch pine is the primary tree and blackjack oak is secondary. There are usually scrub oaks, huckleberries, low-bush blueberries and ferns as well.

Plant communities go through processes of evolution from one type to another. For instance, a pond, as nutrients build up, may evolve into a savanna, then a spong and then a swamp. If drainage is poor, however, a pond may become a bog. Eventually, the bog will evolve into a swamp too: Deciduous seedlings survive the shade of bogs better than cedar seedlings do, so as mature cedars die, they are replaced by deciduous growth. The evolution of uplands leads to the ultimate dominance of oak trees, because the natural ground litter of needles and branches favors the growth of shade-loving oak seedlings over sun-loving pine seedlings.

But man can cause profound alterations in this natural evolution. Dams flood large areas, killing bushes and trees. Dredging and filling destroy lowland communities and increase the likelihood of future flooding. Savannas and bogs are developed into cranberry and blueberry farms. Peat, sphagnum moss and branches of holly, inkberry, azalea, laurel, pine and cedar are collected for horticultural and decorative purposes. Pine and cedar trees are cut for pulp and cordwood. If a cedar forest is clearcut, as it usually is, deciduous trees grow in its place.

Fires are particularly influential. A cedar forest that is destroyed by fire may regress to a savanna or spong, or it may advance to a swamp because maple roots can send up new shoots that flourish in the increased light. When fire sweeps through uplands and burns away underbrush and ground litter, it creates the conditions that favor survival of pines over oaks. Additionally, the destruction of nutrients by fire reduces the area of the lowland pine transition communities and often creates a sharp demarkation between the lowlands and the uplands. As a result of frequent fires, much of the Pine Barrens ecology is on a twenty-five-year cycle.

Fire may be involved in the existence of an interesting type of upland community located away from the rivers—the pine plains, or pygmy forest, of Ocean and Burlington counties. The pine plains consist of a dense field of bushlike trees, mostly pines, growing no higher than a person's waist. Thirty-year-old trees stand no more than 3 or 4 feet tall. One can see the plains from Route 72. The reason for the dwarfed growth has always been a mystery. Explanations include: toxic elements in the soil, microorganisms in the soil, low soil fertility, a hardpan layer beneath the topsoil, insect pests, low moisture and high winds. Yet all of these have been disproved or are now believed unlikely. The only theory that is still viable is fire. Many botanists believe that frequent fires cause the trees to sprout several shoots and grow in a bushy fashion.

Poison Ivy

Poison ivy is dangerous at all times of year. The oily irritant that produces skin blisters and severe itching lies in canals in every part of the plant. If the canals are undamaged, people can touch a leaf or stem without ill effect. But insects may rupture the canals and permit the oil to reach the surface. Even if oil is not transferred directly to the skin, it may be deposited on clothing or equipment and poison the skin later. Furthermore, it is stable for long periods of time, insoluble in water and difficult to wash off. So it would be well for everyone to recognize the plant. Fortunately this is not difficult.

In the Pine Barrens and most other areas of the Northeast, poison ivy grows as a vine. The color and shape of leaves may vary somewhat, and they may or may not be glossy. But some constant characteristics distinguish poison ivy from other plants:

1. The leaves occur in groups of three. The middle leaf has a stem, but the two side leaves do not.
2. The leaves have smooth edges without regularly spaced teeth.
3. Each leaf is asymmetric. Often, one edge is a simple smooth curve, while the other has one or more coarse serrations.

Examining the vine stalk of a poison ivy plant reveals an unusual feature. The vine does not cling by tendrils, like brier and grape, or twine around other plants, like honeysuckle. It clings by means of hairs, which are called aerial rootlets. On young stalks the hairs may be tiny and thinly scattered; on older growth they are thick. Along the Manasquan River, I saw a poison ivy vine as thick as a man's wrist and ten times as hairy growing up the side of a tree. The hairs are noticeable in all seasons. In the fall, clusters of small, white berries help with ivy identification.

The blisters and itching associated with ivy poisoning are believed to be an allergic reaction to ivy oil. As with other allergies, sensitivity increases with exposure. None of the folk remedies one hears about has been verified scientifically. People who contract a mild case may wish to try calamine lotion to soothe the itching, although I have never found it did much good. A cure that I once found effective took place a week after exposure when I happened to spend a day at the seashore. Recuperation usually takes two weeks, but this time the sores dried up by the end of the day—another folk cure! Anyone who contracts a bad case of ivy poisoning should see a doctor. As with other ailments, however, prevention is the best cure.

6

~~~~~~

Animals You May Meet

In general, all animals are not easy to find along Pine Barrens rivers. The noise of paddles in the water, human voices or a canoe striking a log or brushing against leaves is certainly an important, if not the major, factor. Perhaps the lack of camouflage on the open water is another. In my many years of paddling with a group, the only animals I saw—not counting the mosquitoes and deer flies—were small birds, turtles and, on two occasions, snakes. The sole exception occurred with a group of three canoes when we spotted an egret across a pond.

With only one canoe (preferably midweek), the chances of seeing animals are better. As a matter of safety, however, one should not attempt to canoe alone without thorough experience of these rivers; until then, there should be at least four people in every group. Even with a single canoe, one must be alert because animals move quickly and, when still, blend well with their surroundings. One should try to move unobtrusively down a river, paddling firmly but not so vigorously as to churn the water. Also, the season and river may be important. For me, the fall is the best season for seeing animals, and the upper section of the Great Egg Harbor River is the best place.

The evening is a good time to look for animals, and watching helps to while away the long nights in the fall. On one occasion, when I was camping alongside a river, I saw a young deer thrashing through the water and apparently looking for a spot to climb out. It started up on my side, then stopped and must have sensed something amiss, because it turned back, struggled down the river about 10 feet from me, and scrambled over to the opposite bank. Another time, while car camping, I turned the headlights on a fox that was roaming the area. Taking along a flashlight equipped with a red filter, whose light cannot be seen by animals, makes it easier to locate animals at night.

There are many small birds in the Barrens. I am not a birder, but almost anyone can recognize a bluejay and a red-winged blackbird. The most common nesting songbird is said to be the towhee, and, sure enough, it can often be heard singing its characteristic "Drink your teeeee." The whippoorwill is heard all night long in the late spring and summer, as is an occasional owl. During the day one hears the owl-like call of the mourning dove, as well as the bobwhite and an infrequent woodpecker. There are many raucous birds, too. One day my attention was attracted by a flock of crows, and I looked up to see them fussing around something. it was an owl, which, unable to endure the attack in one spot, periodically flew from tree to tree. The sounds of the many bird species vary in sonority, pitch, texture and rhythm, and transmit contrasting impressions. They are all different, yet none seems out of place, and together they are like a musical composition.

Despite the dominance of the towhee as a songbird, my vote for the commonest bird in the Pine Barrens goes to the duck. No matter what the season, not a day of solitary canoeing passes in which I do not see ducks. They flush vertically out of the water in groups of two or three, with one or two complaining quacks, and fly away, sometimes to alight downstream and other times to be silhouetted against the sky. One can rarely get within 20 feet of a duck before it skitters away.

On a clear, sunny day one occasionally spots a turkey buzzard, black with white-tipped feathers, soaring gracefully high overhead. A great blue heron may stand near the shore of a pond or fly low with slowly flapping wings. In the fall, Canada geese fly southward in their customary V-formation, sounding like barking dogs. I have seen a few grouse fluttering through the woods, but only once have I spotted pheasant, sandpipers, woodcocks or whistling swans. Other large birds are rare.

Insects are generally in profusion from late spring until the first good frost of fall. Only two varieties are nasty—mosquitoes and deer flies. Most people are familiar with mosquitoes. A deer fly is the size of a large house fly but is brown and not as fat. Its bite is painful: The victim can actually feel its blood-sucking tube penetrate his skin. Both insects arrive at about the same time, toward the end of May. The deer fly has usually disappeared by September; the mosquito flourishes into the fall. These insects' numbers depend on the degree of dampness of early spring weather. In dry years, they may be less numerous.

Although New Jersey counties have mosquito-control programs, they have not been successful in controlling mosquitoes on rivers and lakes, except for the Maurice River. Most good insect repellents work against mosquitoes but not against deer flies. The deer fly is slow enough to be slapped, and its bite gives warning (unlike the mosquito's). Still, the best preventative is to wear full, loose clothing. My own preference is to avoid the Pine Barrens when the deer flies are out.

Dragonflies, or darning needles, are present in the summer. Some people think they bite, which is not true. They are handsome because of their brilliant colors, and moreover, they eat mosquitoes; so they should be left alone. Butterflies may also be found. A survey indicated that more than ninety-one species live in the Pine Barrens. There are other flying insects. Some of them are attracted to people, but none with injurious intent.

51

Spiders reveal themselves by their webs. Sometimes spider strands span the narrow rivers in June, but they can usually be dodged or brushed away. After a rainstorm, one can admire the delicate pattern of a web supported between two plants with its strands highlighted by clinging droplets of water.

A healthy share of amphibians and reptiles inhabits the Pine Barrens, yet only turtles are seen with any frequency. In the early spring they lie on the ground, catching whatever warmth they can. In the late spring and summer they rest on tree trunks and branches that extend over the rivers. Canoeing along, one can hear the steady plopping sound of turtles falling into the water to avoid detection.

A wetlands animal one almost never sees is the Pine Barrens tree frog, which is on everybody's list of endangered species. Found only here and in two other places in the United States, it is elusive and deserves to be let alone.

Snakes are almost never encountered, and anybody who wishes to avoid them has only to stomp through the woods, making as much noise as possible. Being smaller than people, snakes are eager to avoid a confrontation and quickly remove themselves from any disturbance. They may rarely be seen in early spring in an open area, coiled like a rope to conserve heat.

Although I rarely meet a person river fishing, I have encountered several people who talk about it, and apparently it has a small following. Because the water is acidic, it does not support many varieties of fish. Most fishermen try for pickerel, which thrives in acid water and for which pickerel weed was named. In this region, plant and fish are often found together.

Deer are supposed to be the most frequently observed mammals in the Pine Barrens. This is certainly not true on the rivers, perhaps for the reasons already stated. Of the mammals I have seen, squirrels and chipmunks are the most common, with deer a poor second. Third is muskrat, swimming or scram-

52

bling into holes in the banks. Bringing up the rear are two foxes and a raccoon. Opossums are supposedly found throughout the Barrens, but I have never seen any.

Seeing a fox was the highlight of one canoeing day, and I almost missed it. After paddling by a grassy bank, I heard a rustle in the woods and, turning, saw the animal reclining in the grass and watching me, not more than 10 feet away. After a period of mutual examination, I lost the magic moment by approaching to take a photograph. The fox perked up its ears, turned and moved into the bushes.

Beaver are evident at several places along the rivers. At present they are most common on the Mullica River, where they have constructed a half-dozen or so ponds and lodges. Other signs of their existence can often be found. They topple a tree by gnawing through it, leaving chisel marks in the stump and chips on the ground. Then they eat the bark, and one can find branches on the ground or in the water that are stripped clean. Beaver are difficult to observe, but they can be seen by quiet groups in the early morning or evening; at night they might be heard in their lodge.

Hunting is allowed in New Jersey's state forests, including the Wharton Tract. Deer, small game, ducks and geese are hunted, while beaver and muskrat are trapped. Different phases of the hunting season extend from October through December. Canoeists are safer than hunters, but if you wish to obtain a schedule of the hunting season so you'll know what's going on, write to the New Jersey Division of Fish and Game, Department of Environmental Protection, P.O. Box 1809, Trenton, NJ 08625, and request the latest game compendium.

7

~~~~~~~~~~~~~~~~~~~~~~~~~~~~~~~~~~~~

When Your Bed Is a Bag

There are many campgrounds in southern New Jersey, both public and private. (Most of them are listed in Appendix A.)

For a two-day canoe trip, one can either pack all the camping gear in the canoe and spend the first night on the riverbank, or carry along only the necessities of the day and drive to a campground for the night. Both procedures have advantages and disadvantages. Camping on the river usually contributes more to a wilderness experience, although occasionally one can feel trapped by noisy neighbors. Also, liftovers become difficult because of the extra weight, and the gear must be protected against capsizing and bad weather. Car camping is more comfortable and increases freedom by allowing a different river to be paddled on the second day, but the extra shuttling wastes time, and the campground is often crowded. The choice depends on one's ability and taste, or on certain logistical factors described later in this chapter.

Camping on the River

River camping is risky except at established campgrounds. At one time it was possible to find an isolated, dry spot where one could pull over and quickly set up a simple camp; the Toms and Great Egg Harbor rivers could be paddled that way. But that option has been all but eliminated because of 1) the threat of midnight vandalism; 2) the establishment of state wildlife management areas where camping is illegal (although these areas do protect rivers from development); and 3) development by the state or private landowners for other purposes. Wherever one camps, open fires are prohibited without a fire permit; so if a small beach area can be found where camping is not illegal, it is best to use a cookstove.

At the present time, camping is possible alongside the following rivers:

- Mullica River: Two campsites are accessible by car as well as canoe, and a third is closed to vehicles. Camping elsewhere is prohibited. No more than one or two liftovers should be necessary, but canoes must be portaged across the highway at Atsion. The campsites enable one to canoe on the river for two or three days.
- Batsto River: One campsite, closed to vehicles. Camping elsewhere is prohibited. Except for some possible shallow sections, the river is clear. Two days.
- Wading River: Four facilities, accessible also by car. Camping elsewhere is prohibited. Liftovers are unlikely. Two days.
- Toms River: Dover township has a campsite, but a camping permit must be arranged in advance. Upstream, one would have to scout in advance for a campsite. However, above Whitesville the river is likely to be too clogged with debris for an enjoyable overnight trip. Two days.
- Great Egg Harbor River: A private campground is at the lower end, before entering Lake Lenape. The river below Weymouth is part of the Atlantic County Linear Park System, and the upper section between New Brooklyn Lake and Piney Hollow Road is within the Winslow Wildlife Management Area; in both sections unauthorized camping is

prohibited. Whether camping is possible between Piney Hollow Road and Weymouth should be confirmed by scouting.

Within Wharton State Forest, camping is permitted only at authorized campgrounds. This restriction may seem harsh. But camping is not the same as it used to be. There are more people, and campers are more wasteful, leaving behind unwanted belongings, trash and unsightly campfire pits. Some campers fail to realize how dry the woods can be, especially in the summer and early fall, or how easily a fire can spread by igniting leaves and low growth. Even people who take proper fire precautions are setting a bad example for others if they disobey the no-camping regulation. At the present time, rivers in the Wharton State Forest are patrolled at night, and illegal campers are evicted.

Camping permits must be obtained before camping overnight in any state campground. They can be purchased at the various camp administration buildings during regular hours or acquired ahead of time (prepaid) by mail for an additional fee (see below). In the Wharton State Forest, the administration building is located at Batsto Village; permits may also be obtained at the ranger headquarters at Atsion. You must get a fire permit if you wish to build an open fire, and pets are not allowed in the campgrounds.

On your trip, keep overnight equipment light if you expect liftovers. If drinking water will not be available at the camp, take it with you. In the canoe, be sure that all equipment is tied to the thwarts or wedged in securely. A pack frame is excellent for keeping everything together. Line the pack with a plastic bag to keep the contents dry, or wrap your belongings in multiple plastic trash bags and tie them securely. A small daypack is handy for odds and ends, and you should take along an extra bag for litter.

Car Camping—Public and Private Campsites

Public campgrounds are intended for people camping any length of time from overnight to two weeks. They provide such amenities as tent or trailer spaces, tables and benches, drinking water, washrooms (except in the Wharton State Forest) and toilets. Campsites are situated among trees. Some campgrounds have a cooking fireplace and hot showers. Others have modest recreational facilities. Privately owned campgrounds accept short stays when space is available but cater to people camping from a week to several months. They provide additional features that may include electric hookups, swimming pools, laundromats, playgrounds, recreation rooms, a general store, firewood, ice and planned activities. The sites in some private campgrounds are spaced among trees, but most are open to accommodate large vehicles.

The variability in facilities, atmosphere and cost of the private campgrounds should make it worthwhile to check them out in advance. Also, some private campgrounds accept family groups only.

Reserving a Public Campsite

A mail reservation for a public campsite can be confusing, and it is best to call or write for particulars before the reservation is made, in order to account for any recent changes. A distinction is made, for example, between a "family campsite," accommodating from one to six people, where advance reservations are allowed for either seven or fourteen nights only, and a "group campsite." Fees vary seasonally, and an additional fee is charged for reservations made in advance. The booklet *State Forest, Parks and Recreation Areas Campgrounds* helps to sort out these and other manifestations of our bureaucratic environment and is available at the various headquarters of the Wharton State Forest.

Clearly, the above regulations work against the small canoeing party that wishes to spend only one summer night camped on a river in the Wharton State Forest and likes to plan ahead. If it strikes you as unfair to have to pay for seven nights when you'll be there only one, your sole option is to forget about making a reservation and take your chances on getting a camping permit the day your trip begins. This, however, will prevent an early-morning start on the river because Batsto Village does not open until ten o'clock in the summer (eleven o'clock the rest of the year), and other would-be campers will be trying to get permits, too. Having to get a permit first and then visit a canoe rental agency means you may not arrive at the river until early afternoon. This business may be accomplished more quickly during the spring or fall.

Warning: During the summer all accommodations, public and private, are crowded and should be reserved in advance, if possible, despite any extra expense.

8

Rent a Canoe

There are more than a dozen canoe rental agencies in the Pine Barrens. Some are small businesses run from the family home; others are more commercial and are operated in conjunction with gas stations, motorboat showrooms and tackle stores. A group's choice of rental agency usually depends on its choice of river. That is, a group will use an agency close to the river, especially if it is going to need transportation to the put-in and from the take-out. The agencies that service each river are listed in the river descriptions in this book; Appendix B lists the agencies with their mailing addresses and telephone numbers.

Rental rates vary but are rarely exorbitant. State law supposedly requires that two life preservers be included. But at least one rental agency furnishes none and charges extra for each "life cushion." Others provide life jackets with the canoe and will throw in cushions for a small fee. Additionally, some agencies may insist on an equipment deposit, which is refundable at the end of the day after all gear has been returned in good condition.

Not all agencies haul canoeing parties to the rivers and back, but most do. Prices for this transportation vary and are subject to change.

The total amount for equipment, hauling and tax must be paid before the party leaves for the river.

The people who run the agencies are usually knowledgeable about the current conditions of the rivers they service. They know, for instance, whether a river is too shallow to be negotiable, whether any hazards are present and whether the access road, which is often merely a pair of sandy tracks through the forest, will permit passage by non-four-wheel-drive vehicles. So it is wise to seek their advice and to remain flexible until the last minute.

For a group that wants to be hauled, canoes are stacked upside down on a canoe trailer hitched to an open truck. The canoeists climb into the back of the truck and share it with a jumble of life preservers, cushions, paddles and personal gear. Warning to tall people: now, before the truck leaves, is the time to make sure there is a paddle long enough for you in the truck and to stake a claim on it. For some reason, long paddles are scarce at rental agencies and the ones they provide are too short for anybody more than 5 feet 8 inches tall—until you complain. A paddle should extend from the ground to one's chin. It is a good idea, also, to take along an extra paddle in case of breakage.

Besides variations in size and rates, there are variations in the length of time it takes rental agencies to get groups equipped and leave for the river. A party may be equipped and on its way immediately following the necessary paperwork. On the other hand, it may have to hang around the agency for what seems like forever as the sun rises higher and tempers get shorter. On one occasion during the preparation of this book, I was in a party that was made to wait for nearly two hours. There were only a few customers ahead of us; the easy-going individuals in charge just could not have cared less. As a result of this experience, I nearly dropped the agency from the book. I didn't because I was unable to check out *all* the agencies, and I reasoned that there may be others that are equally poor in this respect.

Reserving Canoes

Renting canoes is popular from May through October, so it is best to make a reservation several weeks in advance, at least for weekends. This requires a deposit. A phone call to the agency telling them the number of canoes needed will reveal the size of the deposit to be sent. In general, one-third of the total fee will be requested. Make sure the deposit gets deducted when the bill is paid on the day of the trip.

The terms for dealing with reservations differ from one agency to another. In pursuit of these facts, three agencies were all asked the same question: "Would you charge our party for the six canoes we reserved if it turns out we need only four?" One agency said yes, unless it was notified ten days in advance. A second said yes, if the weather is good (so the canoes might be rented to another group) and no if it's raining. A third replied, "No, we wouldn't do that. We know it's hard with a group—somebody gets sick and drops out at the last minute." Delightful people! That's the way to keep the customers coming back.

9

~~~~~~

Negotiating the Turns

It is possible for a person without an iota of experience to enjoy canoeing the rivers in the Pine Barrens simply by choosing a skillful partner. But this is not always possible, and sometimes a partner's skill is overrated. Some people, for example, after puttering around a few times on a lake at summer camp, feel qualified to tackle anything and proceed to lead a poor novice astray, often with miserable results.

Perhaps this is overstating the case. After all, the rivers in the Pine Barrens are not white-water streams. The current is not fast, and there are no rocks. On the other hand, the channel is often narrow—sometimes too narrow to turn the canoe around. Even on the wider rivers, turns are frequent, and it can be difficult to keep the canoe from ramming the bank or ricocheting from one side to the other in a desperate attempt to follow the stream's gentle, meandering path. Usually there are two paddlers in a canoe, and the act of paddling generates a torque that tends to rotate the boat; this torque must be counterbalanced. Furthermore, when a canoe turns to get around a bend, it is broadside to the current, and the current tends to drive it against the bank. Then there are logs in or above the water, snags just below the surface ready to hang up the unwary, trees arched over the river with branches in the way, and bushes and brier crowding the banks. With all these things to worry about, novices may miss the purpose of the trip: to enjoy the woods and the water and the pleasure of being in control of the situation.

There are two solutions. One is to canoe for short trips and only on the easiest rivers; the other is to learn how to canoe. Fortunately, the first can lead to the second. Handling a canoe properly on these rivers is not terribly difficult. But it does require time and experience to learn the effect of a paddle stroke on a canoe's movement and the effect of river current on the canoe. Some hints and suggestions follow. Learn what you can, and use what you wish. Experience will take care of the rest.

Equipment

A canoe is usually symmetrical, except for the position of the seats. When completely in the water, it is strong and stable, but at other times, be careful. If it must be hauled over a log, all heavy objects, including people, should be removed to avoid straining the keel. When disembarking, the person climbing out first should *not* drag the boat onto the bank after him, but instead clamp the end between his legs to stabilize it for the other paddler. If he pulls it out before his partner stands up, it will be tippy.

The paddle is the primary means of locomotion. It works to the extent that water approximates a solid medium. By anchoring the blade in this medium, the paddler, progressively using his arms, shoulders, back, trunk and legs, pulls and pushes the canoe through it. The idea is to minimize the movement of the paddle through the water and maximize the motion of the canoe. Success in anchoring the paddle depends on immersing the entire blade, if possible, in the water and orienting it to provide the greatest resistance to motion. The paddle's grip is useful in this orientation. Because it is either flattened or has a dowel attached in the same plane as the

63

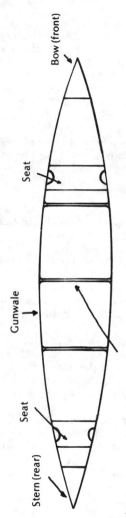

Bow (front)

Seat

Gunwale

Seat

Stern (rear)

Thwart (good for lashing equipment)

Canoe

Blade

Shaft

Grip, flattened to sense blade angle

Paddle

blade, the hand grasping it can sense the blade's direction.

Misuse of the paddle is common, as shown by the broken paddles that line the banks of well-traveled rivers. Recently, the owner of one canoe rental agency lost 400 paddles in a single season because of broken blades. A paddle cannot do much more than it was designed to do. The most common abuse is to use it as a crowbar to pry the canoe off an obstruction. (Using it to push away from an obstruction, though, is not harmful.) A second abuse is to turn it into a campfire implement. Wooden blades may scorch, and plastic blades may scorch, catch on fire or warp.

Canoe rental agencies are supposed to provide life jackets or seat cushions along with their canoes. And private boat owners should be aware that the law requires each person to have a jacket or cushion printed with a U.S. Coast Guard stamp of approval.

Personal gear depends on the season and the weather outlook. People who intend to canoe often should make up their own checklists, but some items that are always useful are:

Waterproof bag or container for carrying gear
Boat shoes
Dark glasses or brimmed hat (to cut glare from the water)
Strap for glasses (to keep them from falling overboard)
Sweater or jacket
Rain gear
Lunch and canteen or water bottle
Litter bag
First-aid kit

Waterproof containers keep things dry in rainy weather and in case of an accident. Everything that you would hate to lose should be put inside these containers. Car keys, wallets and handbags regularly disappear forever in the rivers because their owners don't bother with this precaution. There are waterproof bags and boxes on the market, but in a pinch you can use several plastic bags, one inside the other for the best protection, secured well with a cord. An alternative is one of the lidded plastic buckets available at some fast-food services. The bucket should be tested in advance to be sure the gasket is still good. As for boat shoes, sneakers are fine in warm weather, but at other times wool socks worn inside waterproof boots or some other waterproof covering are preferable. Feet do not get much exercise in a canoe, and if they are also damp and cold, they make the trip unpleasant.

A camera may be added to the above list and, in warm weather, a swim suit and insect repellent. But it is unwise to dress in a bathing suit for canoeing in the Pine Barrens because insect repellents do not work well against deer flies, and increasing the amount of exposed skin may be asking for trouble. On many rivers in early spring and on others year round—the Metedeconk, the uppermost section of the Toms and the upper Great Egg Harbor—canoeists should carry a frame saw and a pair of long-handled pruning clippers.

In cold weather a change of clothing should be carried along in case of an upset. Wool is better than any other material, although a polyester-insulated vest or jacket is good. Down clothing is poor because it loses its insulating property when it gets wet. Cotton is also poor because it dries slowly and wicks moisture throughout the entire garment.

An extra paddle should be placed in the bottom of the canoe as insurance against breakage. Everything else taken aboard should be fastened by loose cords to the thwarts.

Getting Down the River

Whether one sits or kneels in a canoe is a matter of personal choice. The canoe is more stable when you kneel, and the

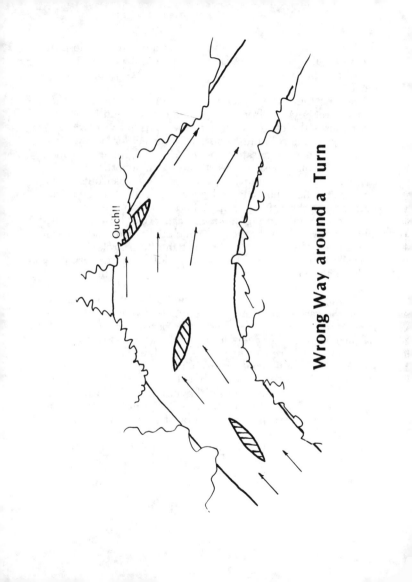

Wrong Way around a Turn

strokes are easier and more efficient, because you are closer to the water. But sitting is much more comfortable. Most people sit while canoeing in the Pine Barrens and take their chances on stability.

The first thing you notice when paddling is that the canoe tends to rotate away from the paddling side; paddling on the right causes the canoe to turn to the left, and vice versa. A person paddling solo must constantly correct for this motion. Two canoeists compensate somewhat for each other, provided they paddle on opposite sides. Paddling on opposite sides also helps to maintain stability. If both paddlers lean out on the same side, the canoe can roll over. So, Rule Number One: Partners should paddle on opposite sides of the canoe.

Even with this arrangement the canoe will turn, in almost all cases, away from the side on which the person in the stern is paddling. This is probably because the stern stroke is farther away from the center of the boat. Paddlers must continually make slight corrections to keep the boat moving in a straight line.

Although turns can be made from either the bow or the stern, they are easier from the stern, also owing to the greater leverage available from the stern. Also, a river current tends to balance turning maneuvers in the stern, which adds slightly to the energy required to make the turn but makes the canoe easier to keep under control. In contrast, the current increases the effect of turns made in the bow to such an extent that the canoe becomes unstable and can gyrate out of control. Thus, Rule Number Two: Steering the canoe is primarily the responsibility of the stern paddler, except of course in a tight turn when the bow paddler may need to help in order to avoid being thrust into the bushes. On lakes and slow-moving streams, which include all the water in the Pine Barrens, the better canoeist is usually in the stern.

When the canoe comes to a bend, the stern paddler may be

able to maneuver the boat to follow the channel, depending on his ability, the width of the river and the current. The problem is how to make the turn rather than run into the outside bank. Merely rotating the canoe leads to disaster, because it will become broadside to the current, and the current will push it sideways into the bank. The best procedure is to approach the turn slowly, keep momentum down and stay toward the inside of the turn to allow room for maneuvering. At this point a stern paddler who knows his strokes can usually negotiate the turn. The bow paddler can help considerably by steering going into the turn and then paddling forward one or two strong strokes to build up momentum coming out of it. Steering keeps the bow out of the bushes, and paddling forward helps keep the stern free.

Paddle Strokes

Many people get by simply by paddling forward vigorously on one side and then the other, switching sides to keep the canoe straight. Sometimes both partners end up canoeing on the same side, with their paddles out of the water as much as in it. This results in much wasted, tiring effort. It is better to follow Rules One and Two and learn the additional strokes necessary for maneuvering the canoe from opposite sides.

Let us suppose that the bow person is paddling on the right and the stern person on the left, and they want to turn the canoe right. This means that the canoe's bow must move to the right, and the stern must move to the left. Either or both execute a "draw" stroke, the stroke that draws the canoe over to the spot where the paddle is plunged into the water. The bow person should keep his paddle as vertical as possible by arching his left arm almost over his head and leaning his body to the right. The blade should go down deep and sweep water underneath the canoe. He ends the stroke by moving his left

69

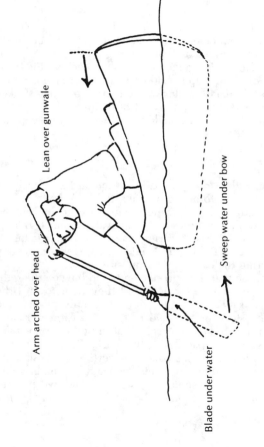

Lean over gunwale

Arm arched over head

Sweep water under bow

Blade under water

Draw Stroke for Bow Paddler

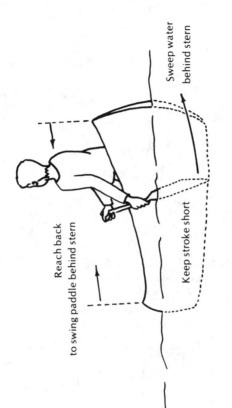

Reach back
to swing paddle behind stern

Sweep water
behind stern

Keep stroke short

Draw Stroke for Stern Paddler

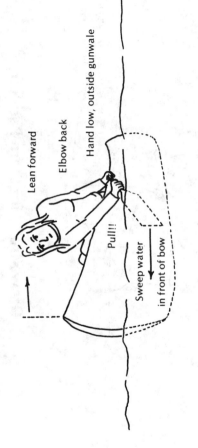

Lean forward

Elbow back

Hand low, outside gunwale

Pull!!

Sweep water in front of bow

Cross-Bow Draw Stroke

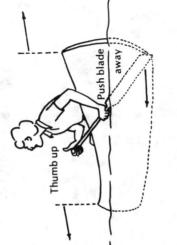

Thumb up

Push blade away

Rudder Stroke

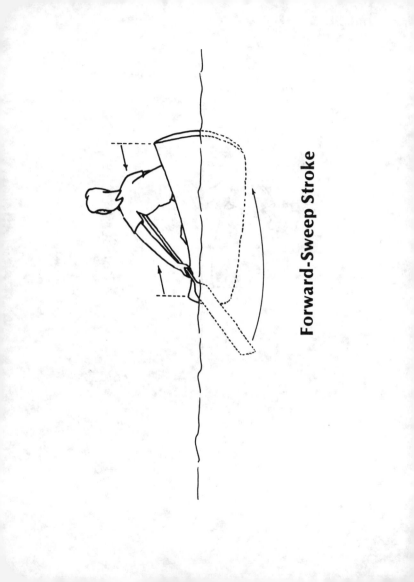

Forward-Sweep Stroke

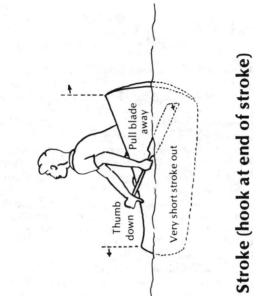

Thumb down

Pull blade away

Very short stroke out

J Stroke (hook at end of stroke)

arm forward and down and his right arm up, so that the paddle blade slices out of the water to the rear. The stern person obtains better control in the draw by keeping his paddle to the rear to sweep water behind the canoe rather than underneath it. The bow stroke is long and steady, and the stern stroke is short and quick.

Now let us suppose that the two paddlers want to turn the canoe left. This means that the bow must move to the left, and the stern must move to the right. The bow person executes a "cross-bow draw," which is a draw stroke done on the side opposite the paddling side. Grasping the paddle in the same way as for a draw stroke (with the right hand near the blade and the left over the grip) and keeping the paddle horizontal, he rotates the trunk of his body to the left. Keeping his left arm low and left elbow to the rear, he places the paddle ahead and to the left, and makes the stroke by leaning forward slightly and sweeping the water from left to right in front of the canoe. This stroke is difficult to execute the first time (and difficult to describe), but it becomes easier. A powerful stroke, it is effective for helping to steer if the stern paddler is weak. It is also a great reducing exercise.

The stern person, for his part, executes a "rudder" stroke, which is the opposite of the draw. He places the paddle against the side of the canoe, with the blade in the water behind the stern, and pushes the blade hard away. Unlike the draw, the stroke need not be short and may even be continued around in an arc until the paddle and canoe almost meet again. This not only turns the canoe but also slows it down and is the most powerful, effective stroke for negotiating a narrow turn. When used as a short stroke, it is a good corrective for keeping the canoe moving in a straight line.

In order to make the usual correction required in the stern, some people merely allow the paddle to drag in the water like a rudder. This works, but more slowly than a legitimate rudder stroke, and it abuses the bow paddler, who has to work harder to maintain forward momentum. At one time the rudder stroke was called a "pushaway," which is more descriptive and distinguishes a useful stroke from a lazy one.

These are the simplest steering strokes. For the stern paddler who wishes to advance, there are two additional strokes worth mastering. Both are intended to be used as forward strokes with corrective components to keep the canoe in line. The "forward sweep" stroke, or "C" stroke, is executed by sweeping the paddle through the water in a wide arc away from the canoe. This stroke turns the stern toward the paddling side, as the draw stroke does, and adds a forward component to increase speed. When rounding a bend, it should be used sparingly because it often makes the canoe move too fast.

The second is the "J" stroke. At the end of a forward stroke, the stern paddler rotates his paddle blade so that the thumb of the hand holding the grip is pointed straight down, and then flicks the blade slightly away from the canoe before withdrawing it from the water. This stroke is difficult to master but is the mark of a competent canoeist because it turns the stern away from the stern person's paddling side while maintaining forward momentum. Perfecting that delicate flick can be awkward, usually because of a failure to point the thumb straight down. (In contrast, the rudder stroke is done with the thumb up.) Having mastered the ability to rotate the paddle blade so that the thumb is pointed down, a person may find that the J stroke is more effective if the blade is rotated continuously during the forward stroke rather than abruptly at the end of the stroke. The alternative to the J stroke is a forward stroke followed by the rudder. But the J stroke is preferable because it is quicker and allows the stern paddler to synchronize strokes with the bow paddler, which makes the canoe move more efficiently. Still, for the novice who intends to remain a novice, the J stroke is not important.

I have assumed that everyone knows the forward stroke and the back stroke, but here are a few hints on improving execution. Keep the paddle vertical; the upper arm should reach over far enough to be directly above the lower arm. This minimizes the tendency of the canoe to turn away. While performing the forward stroke, lean slightly forward; for the back stroke, lean slightly backward. By leaning, you help to bring the muscles of the back into play. When doing a considerable amount of forward paddling—crossing a lake or traveling down a wide river, for instance—relax the muscles for about a second between strokes, or even lay the paddle across the canoe between strokes. The short, rhythmic rest will help keep you from flagging.

Various texts that show additional strokes are listed in Appendix E. In the end, however, each person develops his own variations, so instructions serve only as a framework for experiment.

Water Reading

When the river current is too weak to show the route through a marsh or swamp, you have to follow other clues. One of the best is to watch the flow of bubbles on the water's surface. These rise from organic matter and may occur after the water has been stirred up by paddles. A second clue is to follow the flow of surface dust or leaves. A third, which I have not tried, is to parallel the tree line delineating the river's edge. According to friends, it is a useful guide when one is caught on the river after dark. If all else fails, you may be able to spot a sawed or trimmed log. Often, the route is most difficult to locate in times of high water when the river has overflowed its banks and spread out into swampy woods.

Because the person in the bow can see what lies ahead better than the stern paddler, it is his responsibility to watch

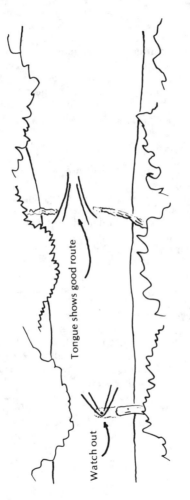

Tongue shows good route

Watch out

River Reading

for obstructions underwater. Sometimes the water is so still that objects can be seen only by direct observation, in which case the bow paddler must be continually on the lookout. But if there is a current, he should be able to see a telltale V-shaped divergence of water around any obstruction and learn to avoid it. When two larger obstructions lie near each other, the water diverging from each meets to form an inverted V or "tongue," which is safe to pass through.

Safety

Although most of the rules of safety are derived from common sense, they bear repeating.

If the canoe rolls over, get out of its way but hang onto the side and, if the water is deep, guide the canoe to a shallow spot where it can be emptied and righted. If there is a chance that the weather may be cold, take along a change of clothing or at least a sweater. Do not paddle alone unless you are sure of yourself and the river; at least four people should make up a group. If you decide to chance it anyway, take along a flashlight as an extra precaution against an immobilizing accident.

On many rivers, logs lying across the water necessitate a liftover—stepping from the canoe onto the log, hauling the canoe over and into the water on the other side, and scrambling back in. The maneuver is occasionally hazardous because of the river's current, branches or slippery spots on the log. Be careful, or you may wrench a knee.

Attempting to run spillways is hazardous and sometimes disastrous. Every gauge station has a low spillway across the river; depending on water level, it is either exposed over much of its length or lies just beneath the river's surface. Water flowing over it creates a small waterfall, and when the water reaches bottom, momentum causes it to curl up and backward, forming a wave that churns back to the spillway in a circular motion. A canoe caught broadside in this churning water will capsize in an instant; anyone thrown into the river between the boat and the spillway will surely be injured. People have lost their lives trying to run spillways at large dams like those at Harrisville on the Oswego River.

A beginner should always portage around spillways unless he is with a group that knows how to run them. For people who are determined to try small spillways when the water level is high enough, the proper method is to paddle straight across with enough momentum to carry the canoe over the spillway should it scrape the top. Both paddlers should move toward the bow first to keep the stern light. But *no one* should try to run large dams, like the two at Harrisville, under any conditions. Give them a wide berth. Approaching close enough to merely take a look, canoeists could be washed over the brink and killed.

What to do in a lightning storm may depend on where you are. I say "may" because I have never seen any instructions on what to do if caught on a narrow river as a storm begins. On a lake you should get to shore as soon as possible and get away from a canoe made of metal. On a river passing through an open swamp or field, where a canoeist is a significant target, the same is probably true. On a narrow river surrounded by trees, however, I suspect that you are just as safe in the water. Once, three friends and I were caught during a thunderstorm while we were trying to clear a section of river. Some of us were standing chest-deep in water, sawing debris, while lightning flashed all around. Although we might have been affected by lightning striking a nearby tree, we felt that the trees as a whole sheltered us from being a target for a direct thunderbolt. Perhaps we were luckier than we knew. If anyone knows for sure, I would be grateful to hear.

81

Canoeing Etiquette

There are no rules of the river for canoeists, such as passing on the left, or having the right of way at a fork. Any observances are based on common sense. Nevertheless, confrontations occur from time to time, and so it would be well to keep some notions of courtesy in mind. When one group wishes to pass another, both should be courteous. The slower party should make way, if possible (no one likes to be tailgated); the faster group should pass only where it is possible to do so without forcing the slower canoe into the bushes. When a group of strong paddlers overtakes a weaker group at a liftover or other troublesome spot, the stronger group should offer to help out. Finally, if you feel that you must have a radio or tape recorder, keep the volume low; or better yet, stay at home.

Winter Canoeing

Canoeing during the winter can be a marvelous adventure, as I hope I indicated in Chapter 1.

If you wish to try it, you might choose the Mullica from Atsion to Pleasant Mills, the Batsto from Hampton Furnace to Quaker Bridge, the Wading, the Toms from Whitesville to the town of Toms River, or the Great Egg Harbor from Penny Pot to Weymouth. If their lakes and dams are not frozen, Rancocas Creek and the Maurice River from Malaga to Route 540 are additional candidates. The easiest, usually requiring no portages, are the Wading and the Great Egg Harbor rivers.

A limited number of public campsites in the Wharton State Forest are open all winter. To learn where they are, write to Wharton State Forest, Batsto, R.D. #4, Hammonton, NJ 08037, or telephone the Superintendent's office there at (609) 561-0024.

10

~~~~~~

River Descriptions

The fourteen rivers that constitute the raison d'etre of this guidebook are divided into four regions: the Wharton State Forest, the northeast, the northwest and the south. The description of the rivers in each district is preceded by a map showing major access roads. Additionally, each river description includes a map showing county roads, useful river identification points, local campgrounds and canoe rental agencies.

Adjacent to each river map, one or more charts show progress points and the river's rating. The progress points indicate the percentage of completion of a river section in terms of canoeing time, which enables canoeists to gauge their progress. For most rivers, the charts are the result of notes taken by me on two canoe runs in the spring and fall of 1974–1975, together with notes taken by Fran and Al Braley on runs in 1989. Where the results are similar, averages are used, and where they are not, deference is given to the more recent observations by the Braleys. The canoeing times are based on the assumption of constant paddling speed without regard for rest stops, portaging over dams or roads, or lifting the canoe over logs, although they do take account of slowdowns due to debris in the water. Clearly, there will **be** distortions because some canoeists will want to paddle slowly at times to admire the riverbank, and because beginners will move more slowly on the upper, narrower and more difficult sections than on the lower sections. Hence the progress points should be regarded only as an approximate gauge.

The river ratings were devised for this guide and have no relation to white-water ratings. They are based on the number of turns in the river, river width and depth, canoeing time and the extent of debris encountered. The "A"-rated sections are easiest and can be enjoyed if both partners in a canoe are novices. The "B"- and "C"-rated sections are progressively more strenuous; one paddler should have enough experience to feel confident in maneuvering a canoe. The "C" rating applies where there is considerable debris, in addition to other difficulties. In some cases two ratings are given, depending on whether the section is canoed in one day or two. If it is paddled in one day, it is considered more strenuous from the viewpoint of canoeing than if paddled in two. (The problems of camping, either on the river or at a campground elsewhere, are of a different nature and are not considered here.)

Each description begins with a brief summary of the distinctive and historical features that characterize the river. It then proceeds in the following order:

Possible routes: For one-day or overnight trips. The one-day trips are intended for people who wish to canoe for a day or to go car camping. The overnight trips are intended for people who plan to canoe with their gear and camp along the river.

Campgrounds: Names of local campgrounds. Addresses and phone numbers are listed in Appendix A.

Canoe rental agencies: Names of local liveries. Addresses and phone numbers are listed in Appendix B.

84

Public transportation: Bus service originating either in New York or Philadelphia, and terminating reasonably close to a canoe rental agency.

Other amenities: Location of nearest hospital. Hospital addresses and phone numbers are listed in Appendix C. General location of gas stations, motels, diners, markets.

Water level: As recorded on a scouting trip, either by noting levels at gauge stations or by measuring the distance from the water's surface to the underside of the lower span of an appropriate road bridge. The correlation between water level and ease of canoeing is not always direct because unexpected problems occur, but it is useful in some cases.

River details: A detailed description of what the canoeist is likely to encounter—river width, turns in the river, debris, foliage and points of interest. The width is expressed in terms of approximate canoe dimensions to give the reader a notion of maneuverability. For instance, a river measuring 1 to 2 canoe *widths* infers that a canoe can just pass through the opening, which is usually blocked by overhanging bushes. A width of 1 canoe *length* (or less) means that the canoe may not be able to turn around. A width of 1½ canoe lengths (or more) infers ample maneuvering space. If the river width is more than 3 canoe lengths, conditions approach those of lake canoeing. The judgments were estimated in terms of a 15-foot canoe. Debris was not considered in estimating river width, and whether the limitations of overhanging bushes were included depended upon the circumstances.

The term "river right," found occasionally in the text, refers to the right side of the river, usually the right bank, as seen when facing downstream; similarly for "river left."

A word of warning: Nature is capricious. Changes are occurring all the time on rivers. Conditions that prevailed when this book was written may be different when you get there; indeed, they may vary from one month to the next. So it pays to check with a canoe rental agency before each trip for the latest river report.

If you should encounter important changes that seem to be permanent, changes that you think should be included in future editions of this book, I would appreciate hearing about them. Please cite page number and line(s), and mail your comments to The Globe Pequot Press, 138 West Main Street, Chester, CT 06412.

Reading the maps: In order to maintain accuracy of scale in the preparation of the maps, it was necessary to segment them. This may lead to some confusion in understanding which direction the river runs and how to pass from one segment to the next. The reader should keep in mind the convention that the name of the river appears on its upstream end, that is, the uppermost edge of the map. The arrows appearing at the ends of map segments show how to pass from one map to another.

WHARTON STATE
FOREST

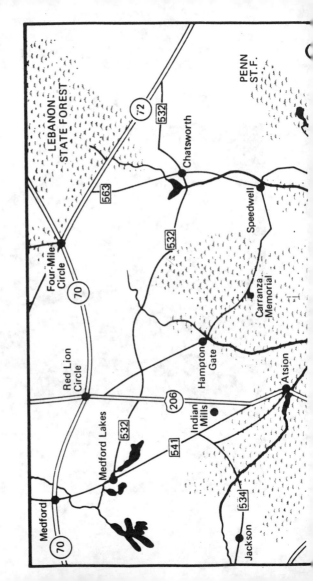

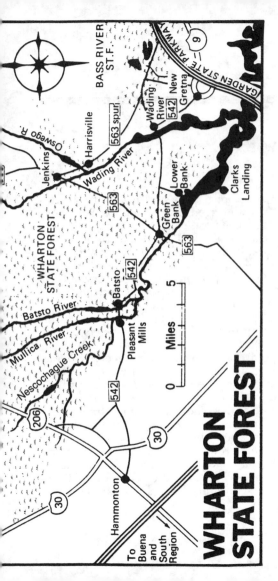

WHARTON
STATE FOREST

11

Mullica River

The Mullica River has a long history in man's affairs. The Lenni Lenape Indians who lived on its banks called themselves the Axions and named the river the Atsayunk, or Atsiunc, while the Lenape who lived on the Delaware River called it the Amintonck. In the early days of British settlement it was called by some people the Little Egg Harbor River and by others Atsion Creek. The portion of the river above Atsion was known as Goshen Creek. The name Mullica came from a Swedish explorer, Eric Mullica, who sailed up the river to what is now Pleasant Mills and established a colony near the town of Lower Bank. In the eighteenth and nineteenth centuries the river was used as an alternative means of commercial transportation to the area's sand roads. The town of Atsion was a major iron producer, and paper was manufactured at Pleasant Mills. At one point along the river there is a pond where bog iron was mined.

The unique charm of the Mullica River comes from its extensive savanna marshes and numerous high, sandy banks that offer ideal places for a snack, sunbathing or a swim. At the upper end the banks are crowded with deciduous trees and bushes, but downstream, below the marshes, the terrain is open except for a few cedars and scattered pines. With its consistent beauty, ease of paddling and isolation from development, the Mullica has to be everyone's first or second favorite river in the Pine Barrens. It would be my recommendation for anyone new to the area.

In recent years beaver have moved into the Goshen Pond area and along the run between Atsion and the old campground. They can be observed by quiet groups, especially in the early morning or evening. Breeding boxes for wood ducks, made of wood or two plastic buckets glued together, have been placed in many beaver ponds.

The segment from Atsion to Pleasant Mills is now designated as a "Wild River," part of the Wild and Scenic River System of New Jersey.

A word about pronunciation: Atsion is now commonly pronounced "At-zigh'un," with the accent on the second syllable. But if you don't want to be taken as a newcomer to the Pine Barrens, slur the second and third syllables together and say "At'zine" as the old-timers do.

Possible routes. The best one-day trip for beginners who intend to rent canoes (including hauling) is between the old Mullica Camp and Pleasant Mills. The run starting at Atsion is no more difficult, but its extra length may be too much for the novice. Nevertheless, those who bring their own canoes should start at Atsion unless they have cars with four-wheel drive or are willing to risk getting mired in the sand on the way to the old Mullica Camp.

At Atsion, putting in directly from Route 206 is hazardous because of heavy automobile traffic. The best put-in location is just off Route 206: Drive a few yards down a small dirt road on the south side of the river toward the ruins of an old mill; at that point, there is a short, narrow path leading back to the river, along which the canoe can be carried.

The trip from Atsion to Pleasant Mills actually makes a good overnight run, with camping at the Mullica River Camp. An alternative trip with a long second day is from Jackson Road (Route 534) to Pleasant Mills, with camping at Atsion Lake. The stretch of river between Jackson Road and Atsion is short, very narrow at the beginning and has many sharp turns. But getting an early start the next day, one can enjoy the morning mist on the lake and finish the trip with little difficulty. The ultimate in casual canoeing is a three-day trip from Jackson Road to Pleasant Mills with overnight stops at Atsion Lake and Mullica River Camp.

Parking overnight at the canoe access at Pleasant Mills is not recommended, owing to numerous incidents of vandalism. Anyone with a camping permit at the Mullica River Campground may park free at the Batsto Headquarters, where the parking area is active and well lit; otherwise there is a nominal charge. The walk to the Pleasant Mills access takes less than fifteen minutes.

Below Pleasant Mills, the Mullica is tidal. Canoes can continue and take out at Crowley Landing, where the state operates a boat ramp off Route 542. This adds about one and a half hours on the river. This could be extended with a side trip up the Batsto to the spillway at Batsto Lake, which would add another one and a half hours. Pleasant Mills to Batsto would take about two hours, including a short walk to or from one's car. As a short day trip, however, the run from the dam at Batsto to Crowley Landing is more attractive.

Campgrounds.
Atsion Lake Camp
Batona Camp
Bel Haven Lake
Buttonwood Hill Camp
Goshen Pond Camp
Mullica River Camp (inaccessible by car)
Paradise Lake Campground

Canoe rental agencies.
Adams Canoe Rentals
Bel Haven Lake
Forks Landing Marina
Mullica River Boat Basin
Paradise Lake Campground

Public transportation. From New York City access is via Atlantic City Coachways. Purchase a ticket to Hammonton and ask the driver to stop at Lake Atsion. Canoes can be rented at the lake from Adams Canoe Rentals. Arriving there in the late afternoon, one can put in at the lake, paddle up to Atsion Lake Camp for the night and start downstream early the following morning. When returning to New York, ask the canoe hauler to take you to the railroad crossing south of Atsion to meet the city-bound bus.

From Philadelphia one may take the New Jersey Transit bus to Mount Holly, then walk to High Street and up High Street as far as Rancocas Road (about two blocks in all) to catch the Atlantic City Coachways bus from New York City.

Other amenities. The nearest hospitals are situated in Hammonton and Mount Holly. Both cities have other amenities as well. Cabins are available for rent at Atsion Lake Camp. There are motels and diners on Route 206 north of Route 70, and a market on Route 206 south of Route 70. A public recreation area with a beach and swimming is at Lake Atsion, across from the Atsion Lake Campground.

Water level. At the Atsion Bridge, there is a gauge on the abutment on the river left on the downstream side, but it may be difficult to read, owing to dirt and water turbulence. The bridge is too large to determine the water level by measuring from the underside of the bridge. An alternative is to measure

93

the height of the lower end of the abutment on the river right, across from the gauge. A gauge reading of 2.80 corresponds to a height along the lower end of the right abutment of about 53 inches. On the spring run the water level was 36 inches, and in the fall it was 57 inches. The canoeing downstream from Atsion is good at both levels, except that at the lower levels, canoes may have to be hauled over beaver dams. This section is generally navigable throughout the year, except in August or September of a very dry summer. The river above Atsion, however, contains less water. It should be satisfactory when the water level at the Jackson Road bridge is 43 inches below the bridge, but at 50 inches, many of the bends in the river would be difficult to negotiate in a 17-foot canoe.

River details from Jackson Road to Pleasant Mills. Initially the width of the Mullica is about ¾ of a canoe length. But within ten minutes, it narrows to 1 to 3 canoe widths for a considerable time, sometimes passing through dense bushes, with very tight and frequent turns. In high water the river overflows its banks, and the channel may be hard to follow. The trees are mostly deciduous, numerous and slender. After a half-hour, the bushes thin out and the river is wider; then the growth is alternately dense and sparse. Debris is minimal, although some liftovers may be necessary in low water. An hour after the put-in, the trees thin out, and stands of grass begin appearing here and there. Then some cedars appear along with leatherleaf bushes and lily pads. Soon the river crosses under the wooden bridge of the old Jackson-Atsion Road. There is a small, sandy bank on the downstream side of the bridge that makes a good rest stop.

After the bridge the river gradually widens to ½ to 1 canoe length; turns are still tight but not as frequent as before. Deciduous trees show up occasionally but are gradually replaced by cedars and pines. Soon grasses become more common,

94

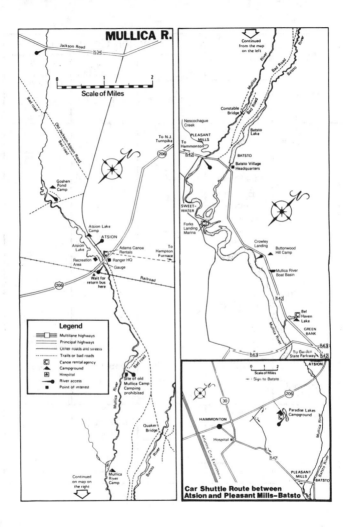

MULLICA R.

Scale of Miles
0   1   2

Jackson Road [534]

Bad road

Old Jackson Road Bad road

To N.J. Turnpike [206]

Goshen Pond Camp

Atsion Lake Camp
ATSION
Atsion Lake
Adams Canoe Rentals
Recreation Area
Ranger HQ
Gauge
To Hampton Furnace
Railroad
Wait for return bus here
[206]

Legend
- Multilane highways
- Principal highways
- Other roads and streets
- Trails or bad roads
- Canoe rental agency
- Campground
- Hospital
- River access
- Point of interest

Mullica River
Bad road
Site of old Mullica Camp Camping prohibited

Quaker Bridge

Batsto River

Continued on map on the right
Mullica River Camp

Continued from the map on the left

Mullica River
Batsto River
Bad road

Constable Bridge
Batsto Lake

Nescochague Creek
PLEASANT MILLS
To Hammonton
[542]
BATSTO
Batsto Village Headquarters

SWEET-WATER
Forks Landing Marina

Crowley Landing
Buttonwood Hill Camp
Mullica River Boat Basin

[542]

Bel Haven Lake
GREEN BANK

[563]
To Garden State Parkway [542] [563]

Mullica River

Scale of Miles
0   1   2
→ Sign to Batsto

ATSION

[30]
HAMMONTON
Paradise Lakes Campground

Atlantic City Expressway

Hospital

[206]

[542]

Mullica River

PLEASANT MILLS
Batsto River
BATSTO

Car Shuttle Route between Atsion and Pleasant Mills–Batsto

Mullica River		Fraction Completed		
Access Points	Landmarks	Jackson Rd. to Route 206	Route 206 to Pleasant Mills	Old Mullica Campgrnd to Pleasant Mills
Jackson Rd.		0		
	Old Jackson-Atsion Rd.	1/3		
	End of spong	1/2		
	Goshen Pond Camp	3/4		
Route 206		1	0	
Old Mullica Campgrnd			1/3	0
	Mullica R. Camp		2/3	1/2
	Gauge & iron bog		3/4	2/3
	Constable Bridge		9/10	4/5
Pleasant Mills			1	1
River Rating		B	A (overnight trip) B (day trip)	A
Canoeing Time, hrs.		3–4	4½–6	3–4

alternating with bushes, which become predominantly leath-erleaf. Gradually the river widens into a "spong," or marsh—an open, dense field of leatherleaf bushes and grasses, framed by distant cedars and pines. Along the edges of the channel grow cranberries, irises and water lilies. The turns become more gentle as the river meanders through the marsh. This is an outstanding area, especially in late March and early April when the leatherleaf bushes are in bloom. Twenty to thirty minutes after the bridge, the spong ends as the river forms again. On the right there is a stopping place that gives a good view of the marsh.

The river is now ¾ to 1 canoe length wide, the banks are firm and crowded with bushes and trees, and the turns are mostly gentle. After a half-hour or so, the banks slowly lower, and the river gradually loses form as it approaches Goshen Pond. Trees, grasses and bushes grow in the water; there are pines off to the left on high ground. The pond itself is small, pretty and lined with pines; bushes and trees cluster in the middle. Goshen Pond Camp is located on the left and is ac-cessible by several sandy roads. There are beaver dams in and downstream from Goshen Pond.

The river leaves the pond at the far end of the camp and is difficult to spot because bushes block the way. A short, cove-like shoreline with two sandy banks indicates the camp's end; the stream passes into the woods just to the right. But its water flows between trees and there is no channel. Although in high water one can force through by bearing left, it is much easier to take out and portage over the left shore, which is a spit separating Goshen Pond and a pool. From the pool a narrow passage of water leads to a point where the river forms a chan-nel again.

Trees line the banks for a short distance beyond the point where the river closes in again, but as the stream passes under a narrow wooden bridge, they disappear and are replaced by a very dense growth of bushes. The channel soon spreads out and the near banks are laden with bushes and grasses. After one passes around an island, Atsion Lake comes into view with Route 206 in the distance. There is an island in a cove on the left, and then one can see small, sandy ramps, which lead to the individual campsites of Atsion Lake Camp. At the far end of the camp is a low, broad ramp that is good for taking out a fleet of canoes. On a windless day about twenty minutes of lake canoeing separate this ramp from Route 206. At the far side of the lake, the canoe must be portaged around the dam and over the highway.

Below Atsion the river is 1 to 1½ canoe lengths wide, and turns are gradual. The banks are firm and covered thickly with deciduous trees and bushes that tend to overhang the water. In a few minutes the river passes under a railroad trestle. Several minutes beyond the trestle, large logs are encountered occasionally; most can be steered around or squeezed under, but one or two may require liftovers, depending on the level of the water. Turns are sharp and frequent. On the banks, cedars are mixed with maples, and an occasional pine is seen in the distance.

From thirty to forty-five minutes out of Atsion, the first of innumerable sandy banks appears on the left, and the turns gradually become more gentle. In another ten to fifteen minutes, the trees thin out, although the bushes are still dense, and the terrain becomes much more open. Two low, flat fields where lichens, moss and a few pines grow are located on the right within ten minutes of each other. In many places the river backs up into grassy ponds. Soon the bushes are replaced by hummocks of tall grasses. In a few minutes the river spreads out into a broad, grassy marsh where the water passes among countless hummocks. There is an excellent place to stop on the right. The ill-defined channel meanders slowly from one side to the other through the open field of water and grasses, lilies and irises. Small maples are scattered here and there, and one usually can see pines growing on higher banks in the distance. Eventually, there is a high, sandy bank on the right, and a few minutes later the banks converge at the end of the marsh. The bank on the left, cleared of bushes, slopes gently up to the site of the old Mullica Camp, a popular place to start canoeing to Pleasant Mills. Camping is no longer permitted here. Be careful of the beaver dam, if it is still there. At low water it could be responsible for a drop of 3 to 4 feet, and boats laden with camping gear might take in water when running it. If necessary, canoes can be carried over on the left.

Bushes and trees crowd the banks again, and branches sometimes overhang the river. There is occasional debris. Ten minutes downstream from the old campground, the frequent turns are the most severe below Atsion. They continue for another fifteen to twenty minutes. Clumps of grasses appear now and then, and the banks become swampy, alternating with an occasional high, sandy bank topped by pines. Nearby there is a beaver dam, and one can occasionally see felled trees whose bark and trunks have been gnawed through. Grasses grow everywhere, mixed with bushes and scattered maples.

After passing several exposed banks, the river begins to spread out into another marsh. It is similar to the previous one but has more maple trees, and the water is quieter, apparently drifting aimlessly. The lazy water, moving broadly through the grasses before a background of pines, is enchanting, as all marshes are; but one should keep one's eyes on the channel, or at least the riverbank, to avoid getting stuck in a shallow area or paddling off in the wrong direction. After meandering slowly one way and then the other, the river tends to flow along a high bank on the left. Soon a tributary bubbles in from the right, and the Mullica River Camp follows shortly thereafter on the left, on a well-marked, cleared bank.

Below the campground the river is 1½ to 2 canoe lengths

wide with a narrow spit of trees separating it from a broad, grassy pond. Ten to fifteen minutes from the camp, there is a low, sandy bank on the right that leads to a field of sheep laurel and blueberries interspersed among pine trees. Cedars, cranberries and pitcher plants line the damp banks.

Soon one comes to a small wooden storage tank next to a platform bearing a water gauge. On the left is the entrance to a small, shallow pond, which may be drained during times of low water. Its bottom is caked with the hard, rusty brown limonite that was the source of iron for the bog-iron industry in the Pine Barrens. Easily accessible to the furnaces at Batsto by both river and sand road, this pond was undoubtedly mined for iron during the nineteenth century.

A half-hour of canoeing separates this pond from Constable Bridge. In this section the river gradually widens to more than 2 canoe lengths. The broad marshes are gone, cedars are infrequent and pines appear scattered along the shore among grasses and low bushes. At several places the banks are high and exposed, sandy beaches lead down to the water. Within sight of the bridge, a low but steep portion of the right bank shows a patch of more limonite.

The run from Constable Bridge to Pleasant Mills takes thirty to forty-five minutes; one can judge accordingly how to allot the remainder of one's time. The river continues to flow broadly and openly with long, meandering turns. Bushes and grasses grow along the edge. The banks are high behind several outstanding sand-rimmed coves, and growing upon the banks is a pine forest. Just past the final beach on the right, there are high, sandy banks on both sides where a bridge once spanned the river, and bridge ruins can be seen on the left. From here to Pleasant Mills takes ten to twenty minutes as the channel narrows to 1 to 2 canoe lengths, and mixed cedars and deciduous trees become dense and overhang the river.

The take-out is located on the left about 25 yards downstream of the highway bridge at Pleasant Mills (just west of Batsto Village) and is marked by yellow rings painted on two trees. People renting canoes from the Forks Landing Marina may continue beyond this point and take out instead at the dock in Sweetwater. Past Pleasant Mills the river broadens into tidal water; the additional paddling to Sweetwater takes forty-five minutes.

12

~~~~~~

Batsto River

Much of the canoeable length of the Batsto River lies within walking distance of the Mullica River, which might lead one to assume that the two rivers look alike. Not so. The Batsto's marshland is different from the Mullica's, it has fewer exposed, sandy banks and it passes through an extensive cedar forest. The Batsto probably has more variety than any other river in the Pine Barrens. Of the four that flow through the Wharton State Forest, it is the least accessible, so it is preferable for people who seek solitude. Additionally, there is almost no wood debris. The sole negative factor is the crossing of Batsto Lake: Because the lake is artificial and shallow in many places, the crossing can be tough in a head wind unless one can feel one's way along the original river channel.

Like the Mullica, the Batsto River was important in U.S. history. Ironworks stood along its upper, middle and lower sections. The rare curly grass fern was discovered near the Batsto. And at one time the town of Batsto was the largest in the Pine Barrens and an important shipping port. In the early 1700s, the British called the waterway the Swimming River, distinguishing it from the nearby Wading River. The name was later changed to Batsto, which is supposed to mean "bathing place" in the Indian language. The Indians, however, may have taken the word from the Dutch or Swedish; the subject is still controversial.

Possible routes. For a day trip, one can paddle from Hampton Furnace to Batsto Lake, but it is a long day and should not be attempted by total novices. A more leisurely trip, which provides time to enjoy the scenery, is from Hampton Furnace to Quaker Bridge or from Quaker Bridge to Batsto Lake. The former is slightly longer but has more variety. The roads to both Hampton Furnace and Quaker Bridge are firm sand, bumpy but generally passable.

Despite the amazing durability of these roads, they cannot always withstand the abuse inflicted by heavy traffic from canoe trailers and off-road vehicles. In the past, some liveries refused to haul canoes to Quaker Bridge, owing to the condition of the road at the approach to the bridge from the south. So it is best to verify the situation in advance, either with a livery (if canoes are to be rented) or at the Wharton State Forest headquarters.

Canoeists putting in at Hampton Furnace might want to visit the nearby ruins of a large stone building that was, perhaps, the original furnace. They are at the bridge, which is about 50 yards upstream from the usual, more convenient canoe access to the river.

The complete run from Hampton Furnace to Batsto Lake makes a good, leisurely two-day trip with an overnight stop at Lower Forge Camp. There is no water at the camp, so take your own.

Upstream from Hampton Furnace, the river flows through an open field that once was flooded to provide power for the ironworks (now gone without a trace). Later the field was used to grow cranberries. The river here can be reached at several places, but the roads are of soft sand and can be troublesome.

Still, putting in at the field provides a pretty ride that adds twenty or thirty minutes to the day's run.

In high water, some people reportedly have run the Skit branch, but where they put in is unknown, possibly they put in from Tuckerton Road after crossing the Carranza Memorial Road.

There is no canoe access at Batsto Village; one must use the access farther up the lake. Campers, before parking overnight here, may first want to check with the rangers at the state forest headquarters in the Batsto Visitors Center for reports of vandalism. An alternative parking area is the Batsto headquarters; it is free to campers with a camp permit and available otherwise at a nominal charge. The walk from the take-out to the village is less than fifteen minutes.

A final possibility is to put in below the dam at Batsto Lake. At some point beyond the dam, the river becomes tidal, and it can be run in both directions. One can then go to Crowley Landing, a boat ramp off Route 542 operated by the state Forest Service; a one-way trip takes about one and a half hours. An alternative is to paddle from Batsto to Pleasant Mills, about two hours by canoe including the short walk back.

Campgrounds.
Atsion Lake Camp
Batona Camp
Bel Haven Lake
Buttonwood Hill Camp
Goshen Pond Camp
Lower Forge Camp (inaccessible by car)
Paradise Lake Campground

Canoe rental agencies.
Adams Canoe Rentals
Bel Haven Lake

104

Forks Landing Marina
Mullica River Boat Basin
Paradise Lake Campground

Public transportation. From New York City access is via Atlantic City Coachways. Purchase a ticket to Hammonton and ask the driver to stop at Lake Atsion. Canoes can be rented at the lake from Adams Canoe Rentals. When returning to New York, ask the canoe hauler to take you to the railroad crossing south of Atsion to meet the city-bound bus.

From Philadelphia one may take the New Jersey Transit bus to Mount Holly, then walk to High Street and up High Street as far as Rancocas Road (about two blocks in all) to catch the Atlantic City Coachways bus from New York City.

Other amenities. The nearest hospitals are situated in Hammonton and Mount Holly. Both cities have other amenities as well. There are motels and diners on Route 206 north of Route 70, and a market on Route 206 south of Route 70.

Water level. A river gauge station is at the spillway from Batsto Lake, on Route 542, although it is unlikely to be a reliable guide to the water level upstream of the lake. In medium-high water, the river is about 105 inches below the bridge at Hampton Furnace and about 56 inches below Quaker Bridge, and the gauge on the upstream side of the spillway should read 2.50 feet.

River details from Hampton Furnace to Batsto Lake. Starting from the spot where the sand road crosses the Batsto River, the river is ¾ to 1 canoe length wide. Turns are gentle, and the banks are low, damp and occasionally swampy. Dense bushes often overhang the water and interfere with passage, but they sometimes draw back in favor of thick grasses or scattered

105

trees—mixed pines, cedars and maples. Behind this shore foliage, the land rises rapidly, and more pines can be seen.

In fifteen minutes the Skit Branch flows into the Batsto from the left, and the river widens to 1½ canoe lengths. Then it gradually becomes more swampy, and cedar trees appear frequently. The foliage is thick along the water's edge. Small islands appear in the middle as the river spreads out into a broad and open swamp. Thirty-five to fifty minutes from the put-in, the river narrows as it passes under a railroad trestle.

The river soon widens again and a narrow, deeper channel weaves erratically around partially submerged rushes and underwater grasses. Moreover, the water tends to be shallow, so care must be taken to pick the best route. Deciduous trees grow densely on the banks, but cedars gradually begin to appear. Blueberry bushes show their deep crimson among green foliage to canoeists lucky enough to be here in the fall. Soon cedars dominate both banks, and the shrubbery is scattered. Cedar is the tallest tree in the Pine Barrens, and when a cedar grove grows undisturbed it becomes so dense that it isolates the river from its surroundings. It even bars the sun from the water, although open, grassy glens full of sunlight may be seen through the trees. By this time the river is 2 to 3 canoe lengths wide and is dotted with low islands of grasses and scrubby bushes. Two small, crumbling wooden docks attest to some former activity.

Eventually, the foliage passes through a long transition. At first, patches of pure cedar alternate with mixed patches of cedar and maple; later, both kinds of trees alternate with scattered pines growing on high ground. Where the banks are firm, they support bushes; where banks are soft, swamp grasses grow. On the right a broad, steep bank leads to an open field of pines and low, scattered bushes that is good for a rest stop.

A few minutes past the steep bank, the cedars begin to thin out. The river becomes very wide, pondlike and swampy, with

106

mixed trees, bushes and considerable underwater grasses. After a turn to the right, there is a small island on the left, behind which the river makes a sharp left turn.

The river narrows to 1½ to 2 canoe lengths and begins meandering through an increasingly marshy area as the pines give way to maples and then to marsh grasses spreading out in a broad field. The open vista contrasts with the isolation of the cedar forest. A narrow, low sandy bank appears on the right, leading to a flat, sandy pine field. This field makes a good lunch spot for canoeists who wish to avoid the upcoming campground. A few minutes later the grasses disappear, the river narrows somewhat and Lower Forge Camp comes into view on a high bank on the left, identified by a sign.

About one minute past the campground, the alert canoeist turns sharply right to avoid a cul-de-sac and soon passes some pilings that are the remains of an old bridge. Somewhere in this vicinity a dam once provided power for the ironworks at Lower Forge; perhaps this was the spot.

The banks are low and swampy, and crowded with bushes, trees and grasses. Pines and cedars can occasionally be seen nearby. The turns are very sharp but soon become gentle again. The river tends to spread out as it passes through trees and grasses to form pools. Small, bush-covered islands begin to appear; the river passes around them, losing its form. There is a great variety of foliage. Twenty to thirty minutes after Lower Forge Camp, a broad, high sandy bank appears on the right. Another fifteen to twenty minutes of canoeing takes one to Quaker Bridge, where there is a fine stand of cedars.

It is difficult to believe, but at one time Quaker Bridge was a popular locality. The bridge across the Batsto was first built in 1772 by a group of Quakers needing a safe crossing to the annual Quaker meeting in Tuckerton. Sometime later, Atsion, Hampton Furnace, Lower Forge, Washington, Martha, Harrisville, Batsto and Tuckerton became thriving communities,

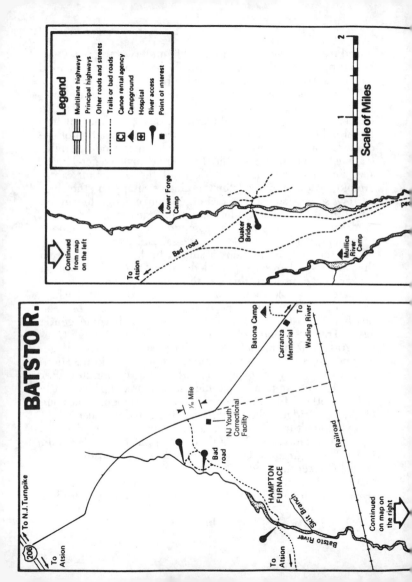

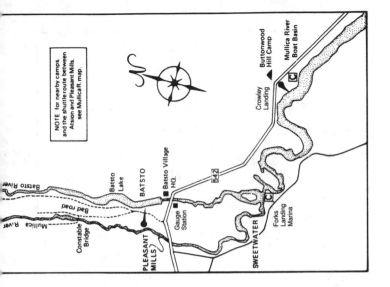

and Quaker Bridge became a crossing for several busy roads. By 1810 the Quaker Bridge Hotel was serving as a celebrated spot for festivals and ceremonies. At about that time, the botanical world was shaken by the discovery of the rare curly grass fern at the base of a local cedar tree; scientists came from everywhere to see it. Now, most of the Barrens towns are mere fragments of their former selves or have vanished altogether. The hotel is gone, the botanists have departed and only the ruins of the old bridge stand as a memorial of bygone days.

An incident that occurred in this area many years ago was used to confirm the existence of the legendary White Stag, which was known to warn of danger. During a heavy, blinding rainstorm, a stagecoach was passing through here at night, when a white stag suddenly bounded into the middle of the road. The driver stopped, and the stag disappeared. But he

Batsto River		Fraction Completed		
Access Points	Landmarks	Hampton Furnace to Batsto Lake	Hampton Furnace to Quaker Bridge	Quaker Bridge to Batsto Lake
Hampton Furnace		0	0	
	Railroad trestle		1/4	
	Sandy cove following dock ruins	1/3	1/2	
	Lower Forge Camp	4/10	3/4	
Quaker Bridge		1/2	1	0
	End of first marsh; channel reforms	3/4		1/3
	Enter lake			4/5
Batsto Lake takeout		1		1
River Rating		A (overnight) B (day trip)	A	A
Canoeing Time, hrs.		4½–5½	2½–3½	2–3

walked on farther and discovered that Quaker Bridge had washed out and that the stag saved the coach from disaster.

Nothing like that could happen now, as Quaker Bridge is a modern structure of galvanized steel. But several of the timbers from the old bridge block the river channel under the new bridge, so canoeists should turn aside into a narrow channel close to the right abutment.

The river continues below Quaker Bridge and spreads out into a broad, meandering channel. Small bush-covered islands seem to be everywhere in a vast open field of water. Some scrubby trees, mostly maples, grow in the middle, while cedars and pines stand on the distant banks. The water drifts, apparently aimlessly, around the islands from one bank to another. Fifteen to twenty-five minutes from Quaker Bridge, a sandy bank on the left shore leads to a good open area where pink blazes on trees mark the Batona Trail, a 30-mile hiking path connecting the Lebanon State Forest with Batsto Village. There is another access to the trail on the left shore ten or fifteen minutes later. Soon, marsh grasses appear more frequently along the edges of the islands. Forty-five minutes to an hour below the bridge, a high, steep sandy bank on the right marks the end of the marsh, temporarily, and the river becomes more defined, with pines and bushes on firm banks. Several more banks are sandy and make pleasant places to stop.

For a half-hour the turns in the river are sharper; then the bushes appear only in patches, and the water spreads out once again. Small but dense patches of tall, dark cedars are scattered over the marsh, contrasting with the flat, yellow fields of grasses. The marsh continues for forty-five to sixty minutes with frequent meandering turns. But toward the end, the turns become more gentle, and long, straight stretches lead down a corridor bounded by cedars. At the end of the last straight passage are several islands of bushes, followed by the upper end of Batsto Lake.

111

There is often a headwind on the lake, but by staying to the left initially it is possible to minimize the effects. The spots where rushes grow out of the water and low stumps protrude indicate shallow areas and should be avoided. Under normal conditions it might take twenty or thirty minutes to paddle to the take-out. The take-out is located about halfway down the lake on the right shore, a few hundred yards past a point of land and barely within sight of Batsto Village. It is marked by yellow bands painted around two tall pine trees. There is a parking lot, and vehicles can back down to the lake for easy canoe loading. A sign is posted in the middle of the lake.

Paddlers who wish to take out at Crowley Landing may continue to the dam, where they are permitted to carry around the old sawmill on the right. But don't plan to stop at the village: State Division of Parks and Forestry officials do not allow canoes to land there.

13

~~~~~~

Wading River

The Wading is the most popular river in the Pine Barrens, and it is rivaled only by the Delaware in state-wide popularity. Indeed, on weekends during the height of the summer season, it may well be the most densely packed river in the world, floating several hundred canoes within its narrow borders. The Wading's fame results from several factors: comparatively easy canoeing; convenient access to put-in and take-out, with a short car shuttle between those points; four campgrounds, all accessible by car; and a pretty riverbank sporting diversified foliage. Canoeing in winter is ideal because of an absence of debris and a frosty solitude. A friend and I recently spent a brisk, sunny day in December on the Wading, drifting down the dark water and listening to waves from our canoe lapping against ice in coves along the shore.

The Wading River was once noted for its many examples of Pine Barrens savanna, or grass marsh, but most of the larger marshes have been turned into cranberry and blueberry farms. The town of Speedwell (named after a wildflower) is the former site of an iron furnace; it is also the place where the writing desk was made on which Thomas Jefferson wrote the draft of the Declaration of Independence. At one time the Wading River was known as Speedwell Creek.

Possible routes. The best canoeing section of the Wading River lies between Speedwell and Beaver Branch. Upstream from Speedwell is a chain of cranberry bogs; canoeing through them is messy for paddlers and a nuisance to the landowners. There is no good take-out in the town of Wading River, so continuing beyond Beaver Branch is not recommended.

Although experienced paddlers can easily make the run from Speedwell to Beaver Branch in a day, most people prefer a more leisurely journey. Taking out at Evans Bridge shortens the trip by one hour. Briefer trips run from Hawkin Bridge to Beaver Branch, and from Hawkin Bridge to Route 563. The latter makes an especially easy and beautiful afternoon ride.

Because the state prohibits access to its campgrounds by anyone not actually camping in them, day trippers may not put in at Hawkin Bridge Camp but instead must put in at Hawkin Bridge itself where it crosses Tulpehocken Creek before flowing into the Wading River. There is no adequate access to Godfrey Bridge Camp for day trippers.

A casual overnight run can be made by stopping off at one of the riverbank campgrounds.

Campgrounds.
Batona Camp
Bodines Field Camp
Godfrey Bridge Camp
Hawkin Bridge Camp
Wading Pines Campground

More remote, but still within reasonable distance, are:
Bass River State Forest
Bel Haven Lake
Buttonwood Hill Camp
Lebanon State Forest

Canoe rental agencies.
Bel Haven Lake
Forks Landing Marina
Micks' Canoe Rental
Mullica River Boat Basin
Pine Barrens Canoe Rental
Wading Pines Campground

Public transportation. None.

Other amenities. There are no overnight accommodations for noncampers in the vicinity of the Wading River. Micks' Canoe Rental has a gas station. A general store and gas station are in Chatsworth and on Route 542, ⁶⁄₁₀ of a mile west of Route 563. There is a hospital in Hammonton.

Water level. At Speedwell the water was 22 inches below the bridge in the spring and 26 inches in the fall. That 4-inch difference was quite significant because the water level, although average in the spring, was very low in the fall. Some normally swampy areas had become mud flats. One cause may have been a withholding of water by cranberry growers upstream; when this happens, the level of the river after a rainstorm does not rise perceptibly. Nevertheless, it is rare that the Wading is not canoeable. If in doubt, phone ahead or ask at one of the local canoe rental facilities.

River details from Speedwell to Beaver Branch. As at most put-ins, there is a pool of water at the Speedwell bridge. This particular pool is created by a barrier of debris and leaves that form a chute, downstream of which there are some overhanging branches on the right. They are hazardous in fast water and should be anticipated.

The river narrows to about ¾ of a canoe length for a few

115

minutes and then widens to 1 or 1½ lengths. The banks are low and either damp or swampy. Bushes are thick and deciduous—mostly sweet pepperbush—and overhang into the water, though not severely. The trees are deciduous also and arch high overhead, keeping the river shaded and cool. Turns are gentle and moderate in frequency. In a half-hour the trees tend to diminish in size, and the bushes become thinner. Damp to swampy areas covered with marsh grasses can be seen through the trees. Turns are sharper, then more gentle. Grasses gradually become evident, although there are usually bushes on one side or the other. An occasional pine tree or flat field of pines extends to the riverbank. Cedars are rare. On the left bank only a thin stand of trees may separate the river from a cultivated field of blueberries or cranberries. Soon one comes upon a clearing on the left where a wooden culvert carries water back to the river from an irrigated field.

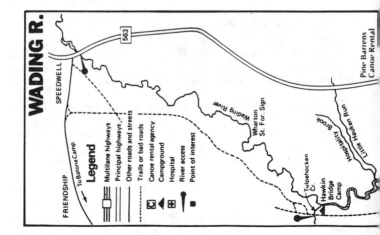

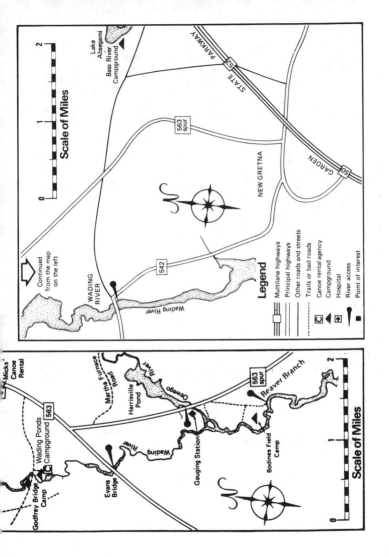

Scale of Miles

Lake Absegami
Bass River Campground

STATE 72 PARKWAY

563 spur

NEW GRETNA

GARDEN 50

Continued from the map on the left

WADING RIVER

542

Wading River

Legend

Multilane highways
Principal highways
Other roads and streets
Trails or bad roads
Canoe rental agency
Campground
Hospital
River access
Point of interest

Micks' Canoe Rental

Godfrey Bridge Camp
Wading Ponds
563 Campground

Martha Furnace Road

Harrisville Pond

Oswego River

563 spur Beaver Branch

Evans Bridge

Wading River

Gauging Station

Bodines Field Camp

Scale of Miles

Wading River		Fraction Completed		
Access Points	Land-marks	Speedwell to Beaver Branch	Speedwell to Evans Bridge	Hawkin Bridge to Evans Bridge
Speed-well		0	0	
	Enter Wharton State Forest	1/4	1/3	
Hawkin Bridge		1/2	2/3	0
	Little Hauken Run		3/4	1/3
	Godfrey Bridge & Camp	2/3		1/2
Evans Bridge		3/4	1	1
Beaver Branch		1		
Wading River				
River Rating		A (overnight trip) B (day trip)	A (overnight trip) B (day trip)	A
Canoeing Time, hrs.		5–7	4–5½	1¼–3

The river turns right and passes into woods. The banks occasionally lead to a flat pine field on the left or right. Sometimes the sand road paralleling the river on the right can be seen. The amount of debris in the water is moderate, but it is rarely difficult to work around. For the next two hours there is considerable variation in scenery—swampy banks with maples and bushes or grasses, higher sandy banks covered with scattered pine trees and low, dry shrubbery, and marshes. The high banks make good places to stop for a rest or a snack. The river's meanderings are also varied—sometimes gentle, sometimes very sharp. From one to one and a half hours out of Speedwell, the boundary to Wharton State Forest is crossed, as indicated by a sign. Soon one comes upon two very high, steep banks on the left shore, two minutes or so apart; the first is about 25 feet high, the second somewhat lower. The reddish yellow of their exposed sand contrasts with the lush green of the surrounding bushes.

The terrain gradually becomes more open. Cranberries are prominent along the banks, showing tiny rocket-like flowers in the spring or bright red fruit in the fall. In times of medium to high water, the river often forms ponds along the swampy shore. Fifteen to twenty minutes past the two high banks, a broad, shallow marsh appears on the right, filled with grasses and bordered by pines.

Next there are several sandy banks that lead to excellent resting places in the pine- and shrub-covered sands. In between, the shore is swampy and overgrown with an increasing quantity of coarse marsh grasses. More ponds appear; they are usually small, but there is a large one on the right with some isolated dead trees in the middle. The river has widened somewhat, to 1½ to 2 canoe lengths, and meanders in a seemingly aimless way. Some cedars appear along the banks; occasionally there is a fine stand of them.

A few minutes after passing some small islands, Hawkin Bridge Camp (marked by a sign) comes into view on a high bank on the right shore. Next to the camp, the Tulpehocken

Creek flows into the Wading, and a few hundred yards upstream on the creek is the Hawkin Bridge. There canoes can be put in or, in an emergency, taken out.

If the water level is high enough, a fine side trip can be made by following the Tulpehocken Creek upstream. I tried it on my spring run when the water level was marginal, and I did more poling than paddling. The best time to do it is after a spring storm. Even then, paddling upstream is not nearly as easy as paddling downstream, but the passage through the marshy wilderness is well worth the effort. On both sides are impenetrable stands of cedars, with cranberries on the damp banks. In the middle of the creek grow grasses, rushes and, in the spring, the smooth, white, yellow-tipped shanks of golden club. Once I saw an egret standing near the opposite shore. Unfortunately, someone recently started a fire near the bridge; many cedars were burned before the fire was brought under control. The blackened area now serves as a reminder of someone's negligence.

Below Hawkin Bridge Camp, the Wading River becomes much straighter and slowly widens to 2 canoe lengths or more. Rushes and grasses grow in the water. The banks are usually high, sandy and firm, but in some places they are low and marshy. Both deciduous and evergreen bushes are present, and cranberries are plentiful. Trees are generally thinly scattered. There are many excellent places to stop and swim or enjoy the view over the water from a high bank. There is no shade over the river.

Thirty to forty-five minutes past the camp, some remnant pilings of an old bridge protrude from the water. Shortly thereafter, a tributary, the Little Hauken Run, flows into the Wading on the left, passing through a thick stand of trees. In another ten to fifteen minutes, a canal appears, also on the left, draining water from a nearby cranberry bog. Within the next half-hour one arrives, under a dense stand of cedars, at Godfrey Bridge and Godfrey Bridge Camp. Only those camping here are allowed to put in or take out via the sandy ramps at the beginning and end of the camp; all other canoeists must continue on.

Past Godfrey Bridge Camp, Wading Pines Campground can be seen through trees on the left; following a left turn, there is access to this campground via a narrow canal. Below the spot where the canal flows back into the river, the river widens and the cedars thin out. There are a number of good sandy banks for rest stops. The river becomes very wide and swampy with grasses outlining the meandering channel in times of low water. Pines and cedars grow along the shore. Past an island, a spit juts into the river from the right; on the spit, there is a fine sandy bank with an excellent view. At one time there was a wooden dam here for a sawmill and gristmill; in times of very low water the remains of the dam are revealed. Several islands later the river crosses under Evans Bridge, thirty to forty-five minutes after Wading Pines Campground.

Below Evans Bridge a set of crumbling pilings marks the position of an old bridge. The river is wide and meanders continuously. Twenty to twenty-five minutes later, there is an island; twenty minutes farther on, another set of pilings. Shortly thereafter, a narrow channel of the Oswego River enters on the left, followed several minutes later by the Oswego itself. After ten to fifteen more minutes one arrives at Bodines Field Camp, which is on the left and is well marked by a sign in the water. Beaver Branch, the take-out spot for noncampers, is reached by paddling another fifteen or twenty minutes and is marked by a sign and a large yellow blaze on a tree. The area is well cleared and is easily spotted from the river.

14

~~~~~~

Oswego River

It is difficult to make absolute judgments regarding the rivers in the Pine Barrens, but the Oswego River is a prime contender for the prettiest. Except for the final push when one must plow across Harrisville Pond, it is striking from one end to the other. The beginning passes through a cedar bog that is larger than bogs on the other rivers, the middle is graced by the open panorama of Martha Pond, and toward the end, before Harrisville, there is a short stretch of mixed woods similar to that on the lower Wading River. It is not, however, a good river for beginning canoeists because most of it is shallow and requires careful steering to avoid running aground and having to haul the canoe over beds of sand and gravel. Martha Pond is very shallow and can be strenuous to paddle in a headwind.

Despite its difficulties for beginners, the river is very popular. Canoe liveries use it extensively when the water is adequate. Harrisville Pond and Oswego Lake are active for picnicking and swimming, and the road over the dam at Oswego Lake is often crowded with off-road vehicles that use the road east of the dam. Experienced canoeists may want to use the river on weekends only when livery operators say the water is low.

Appropriately, the Oswego was called the Wading River in the days when the present Wading River was called Speedwell

Creek. Even today some road maps identify the Oswego as the east branch of the Wading River. Where the present name came from is in dispute. Some authorities believe Oswego is an Indian word derived from the phrase *on ti ahan toque,* meaning "where the valley widens" or "flowing out." Others contend the Oswego was named after the Swago Saw Mill, which was built at Martha around 1741 before the construction of the ironworks. Nearby was the Old Swago Swamp, hence the contraction Oswego. Swago seems to have been a provincial English word that was corrupted from "swag," meaning "low, swampy ground."

During the days when industry flourished in the Pine Barrens, the Oswego boasted two busy towns—Martha, the site of a large iron furnace, and Harrisville, where paper was made from salt grass harvested from the lower Mullica River.

Possible routes. Camping is not permitted along the Oswego River, so only day trips are possible. One may paddle from Oswego Lake to Harrisville or continue on to Bodines Field or Beaver Branch after portaging over the Harrisville dam. There is a possible take-out at a sand beach just before the bridge at Martha Furnace. But because it makes the trip rather short, it is better regarded as a take-out for emergencies. Canoeing from the Martha Furnace bridge to Harrisville Road ordinarily takes forty minutes to an hour.

At one time a sign to Oswego Lake was posted at the turnoff from Route 563, but it is gone at the present time. Heading north from Micks' Canoe Rental, the turnoff is the first road to the right, at the sign for the Rutgers Research Center.

Upriver, the section between Sim Place and Oswego Lake has been canoed in high water, but the local property owners have not been friendly. When I first tried this section, the sand road from Oswego Lake to Sim Place was closed. It is still closed, barricaded and posted. Someday it may be open; if it is, anyone wishing to try his luck should consult the Oswego Lake and Woodmansie USGS quadrangles.

According to reports, vehicles left near the put-in at Oswego dam have been vandalized. Parking is safer in the picnic area parking lot in Penn State Forest, which is on the north side of the lake. Paddling across the lake and portaging to the river requires about twenty minutes. Also, anyone leaving a car at Beaver Branch should park well clear of the passageway to the river, in order to avoid the risk of damage from canoe trailers; this take-out is heavily used by liveries for both the Wading and Oswego rivers.

Campgrounds.
Batona Camp
Bodines Field Camp
Godfrey Bridge Camp
Wading Pines Campground

More remote, but still within reasonable distance, are:
Bass River State Forest
Bel Haven Lake
Buttonwood Hill Camp
Lebanon State Forest

Canoe rental agencies.
Bel Haven Lake
Forks Landing Marina
Micks' Canoe Rental
Mullica River Boat Basin
Pine Barrens Canoe Rental
Wading Pines Campground

Public transportation. None.

Other amenities. There are no overnight accommodations for noncampers in the vicinity of the Oswego River. Micks' Canoe Rental has a gas station. There is a general store and gas station in Chatsworth and on Route 542, $\frac{6}{10}$ of a mile west of Route 563. There is a hospital in Hammonton.

Water level. In the spring when I ran the river, the water was 29 inches below the dam at Oswego Lake, and in the fall it was 33 inches. At the fall level it was quite shallow. As on the Wading River, upstream cranberry bogs divert much of the water during dry periods in the autumn, so a rainstorm following a drought may not raise the river level significantly.

There is a gauge station below the dam at Harrisville. I did not take a reading there on my fall trip, but in the spring the reading was 3.12 feet on the upstream side of the spillway and 2.10 feet on the downstream side. When the Braleys ran the Oswego, water was high, about 22 inches below the dam at Oswego Lake. Readings at the gauge station at Harrisville Pond were 3.00 feet on the downstream side and 3.20 feet upstream.

River details from Oswego Lake to Beaver Branch. Following a broad, swampy pond just below the dam, the river narrows to 1 or 2 canoe lengths, depending on the water level, and there are gentle turns between firm banks of medium height. Trees, mostly white cedars, pines and some maples, crowd the shore. Interspersed are numerous bushes including cranberries. The riverbed of coarse sand or gravel is usually shallow, occasionally to the extreme, and on sunny days glows a rich shade of burnt orange. Sand bars narrow the channel considerably and are sometimes just below the surface of the water, causing many ripples. One should watch carefully for the darker water and the narrower, more regular bands of ripples that indicate more depth. Long, green underwater grasses

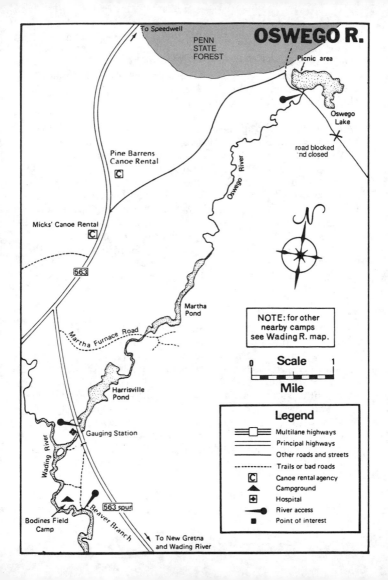

OSWEGO R.

PENN STATE FOREST

To Speedwell

Picnic area

Oswego Lake

road blocked and closed

Oswego River

Pine Barrens Canoe Rental

Micks' Canoe Rental

563

Martha Furnace Road

Martha Pond

NOTE: for other nearby camps see Wading R. map.

Scale

0 _____ 1

Mile

Harrisville Pond

Wading River

Gauging Station

Bodines Field Camp

563 spur

Beaver Branch

To New Gretna and Wading River

Legend

▭▭▭	Multilane highways
═══	Principal highways
───	Other roads and streets
- - -	Trails or bad roads
C	Canoe rental agency
▲	Campground
⊞	Hospital
●—	River access
■	Point of interest

Oswego River		Fraction Completed	
Access Points	Landmarks	Oswego Lake to Beaver Branch	Oswego Lake to Harrisville Pond
Oswego Lake		0	0
	Concrete block bldg.	1/3	2/5
	Martha Pond	1/2	3/5
Martha Rd. Bridge		3/5	3/4
	Enter Harrisville Pond	2/3	9/10
Harrisville Pond Beach			1
	Dam & spillway	4/5	
	Bodines Field	9/10	
Beaver Breanch		1	
River Rating		B	B
Canoeing Time, hrs.		4–5	3–4

flow and spread downstream with the current. Rushes grow in the river and along the muddy shore.

The banks gradually become lower, the pines thin out and

127

the cedars become very dense and extremely tall—first on one bank, then the other, eventually dominating both shores and forming a high, narrow evergreen corridor. Few bushes survive along the banks except for occasional sweet pepperbush or inkberry. This is a cedar bog and very quiet. Sometimes one hears the trees creaking in the wind. The sky and dark silhouettes of the trees are reflected off the quiet water, and the ripples set up scintillations of light and shadow.

The river broadens to 3 or more canoe lengths in still ponds, where lily pads spot the surface. The current is mainly very weak. There is little or no debris, the chief hazard being sand bars. The cedars thin out occasionally, and then the sky is more open; sometimes maple trees hang over the river. The channel makes a few sharp turns. One to one and a half hours from the put-in, a sandy beach appears on the right next to a canal returning water from a cranberry bog. The beach leads to an open, flat field of pines, scrub oaks and various low bushes. This is a good spot to stretch one's legs.

A brief passage of sharp turns follows, and the current increases temporarily. The cedars alternating in patches with deciduous trees and pines resembles the growth on the lower Wading River. Soon the river turns sharply left at the spot where another canal on the right, bounded by piles of sand, diverts water to another cranberry bog. At times of low water, the passage beyond this point is shallow until the spot where the diverted water is returned to the river. In a few minutes a broad, graded gravel beach with a white cinder-block house appears on the right; it is posted with No Trespassing signs. Soon the canal from the second bog rejoins the river from the right. The river becomes deeper, with occasional sharp turns. Tall stands of cedars appear on either side, and a few minutes later the river broadens and enters Martha Pond.

The pond is an open area dotted with cedar- and bush-covered islands of assorted sizes. Pines and cedars crowd the shore. Because it is extremely shallow, one must pick one's way through underwater grasses. Following the right shore seems as good a route as any: it occasionally goes around an island that blocks the view, but otherwise the scenery is quite open. After the second island a canal that was once used to withdraw water from the pond can be seen on the left. The pond narrows and broadens several times as one canoes past more islands, and then it becomes very wide, and the islands turn into grass-covered sand bars. On the outside bend of a sharp right turn, there is a cleared area that leads up a sand "staircase" to Calico Ridge. It was formerly a state camp but now may be used as a rest stop in the event of a strong head-wind. The water is still very shallow, and it contains many tree stumps as well as sand bars. The pond soon bears left, with the deepest water near the right shore. Muskrats and sandpipers can sometimes be seen, and numerous pitcher plants grow along the left shore. In a few minutes the pond ends as the river makes an abrupt right turn. Then the river turns left immediately to face an excellent sandy beach. After another turn the river flows under the old bridge at Martha Furnace, which is accessible from the Route 563 Spur.

A community of about 400 people once thrived on the fortunes of the ironworks at Martha Furnace. The pond provided power to operate machinery. Today not much remains, except for buried ruins of the furnace, as one can see by taking a pleasant walk along the sand road that leads to the town site. And there is other recreation: the river here is very deep, so during the summer carloads of people enjoy a dip in the best swimming hole in these parts.

Just past the bridge several islets are lined across the river. The channel then narrows to 1 canoe length between firm banks of medium height covered with pine and cedar. For about ten minutes, the river runs perfectly straight through columns of trees. This is such a contrast to the numerous turns everywhere else that one suspects it is part of a canal that was intended to carry wares between Martha Furnace and Harrisville.

The banks become lower, the trees thin out and the river gradually widens. Soon there is a sand bank 20 feet high on the left, followed in a few minutes by another high, sandy bank and beach. Immediately after on the left, the shore bulges with mountain laurel blossoms in the spring. In another few minutes, one reaches the top of Harrisville Pond; there is a good stopping place on the left bank for viewing the lake or taking a final rest. Paddling across takes twenty or thirty minutes.

For years Harrisville Lake was held back by a wooden dam. Because it was breaking down, one could have a fine ride on the water spilling over it. But in 1974 it was replaced by a dam of concrete and a second, smaller spillway on the right. The broad take-out area is located between the dam and the spillway but is closer to the spillway.

The journey may be continued, either to Bodines Field for camping or to Beaver Branch, by portaging over the main dam on the left. The gauge station situated a few yards past the highway bridge should be lined over because there is rarely enough water to run it. ("Lining" a boat means to walk along the riverbank and gently guide the boat down the river by grasping the ropes (or lines) attached to the bow and to the stern. Keep it close to the bank in order to maintain control. If the canoe has no ropes or if they are too short, haul it out of the water and carry it around the obstruction.) The river is then wide and shallow, but gradually it narrows to 2 canoe lengths. About five minutes after the gauge station, the river turns left around a cleared picnic area. Straight ahead is a narrow channel that is a cutoff to the Wading River. By remaining on the main channel of the Oswego, one reaches the Wading only a few minutes later. Ten to fifteen minutes later, Bodines Field

Camp can be seen on the left and is marked by a sign in the water. The take-out spot for canoeists not camping there lies fifteen to twenty minutes farther downstream, also on the left, and is marked by a sign, "Beaver Branch," and by a large, yellow blaze on a tree. The area, which is well cleared, is easily spotted.

NORTHEAST

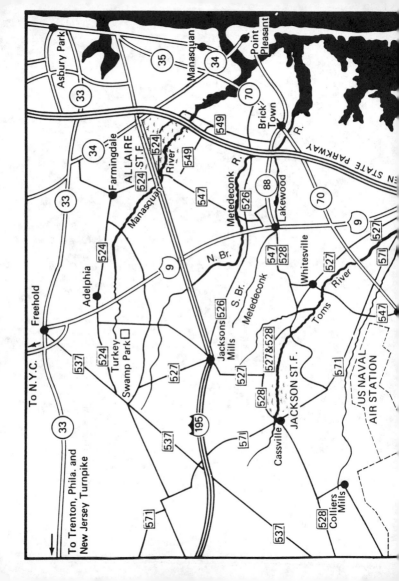

THE NORTHEAST

Seaside Heights

37

Toms River

9

Lanoka Harbor

Forked River

9

Barnegat

532

Waretown

Oyster Creek

530

Cedar Creek

GARDEN STATE PARKWAY

Wells Mills Park

532

72

530

532

Bamber Lake

Whiting

532 72

72

70

LEBANON STATE FOREST

To Northwest Region

MIL. RES.

532

563

Chatsworth

72

To Wharton State Forest

Miles

0   5

15

~~~~~~

Nescochague Creek

Nescochague Creek is probably the least known, least used and most unspoiled of the canoeable streams in the Pine Barrens. It is a tributary of the Mullica River, formed by the confluence of two creeks downstream from the Paradise Lake dam. For much of its length it is the southwestern border of Wharton State Forest. Nescochague was pronounced "Nes-ka-hage" by a ranger at Atsion and "Nes-ka-shog" at Paradise Lake Campground, so take your pick.

Albertson Brook and Great Swamp Branch form the Nescochague. They are barely noticed along Route 206. Albertson Brook fed one of the old cranberry bogs at what is now Paradise Lake. The dam at Paradise Lake is reported to be the oldest dam in the area, and the remains of one of the old berry sorting houses can be seen in the campground.

The charm of the Nescochague is the feeling of remoteness that one perceives as it flows through rarely visited deciduous cedar and pine forests. Few signs of human intrusion are visible between Paradise Lake and the confluence with the Mullica River. It is almost free of litter, and let us hope it stays that way.

Possible routes. For most people, the best run is from Paradise Lake to the Mullica River take-out at Pleasant Mills. It

136

requires about three to four hours of paddling. Alternately, a canoe could be put in at the old steel bridge (denoted here as Sand Road Bridge) on Albertson Brook about 9/10 of a mile from Route 206. To get there from Route 206, turn onto the marked road to Paradise Lake Campground for about 6/10 of a mile. Turn left (north) on a narrow woods road. Follow this to a one-car turnaround at a steel barricade 40 feet from the brook. From the put-in here to Pleasant Mills the creek has been cleared by members of the South Jersey Canoe Club. Don't bother with the short section from Route 206 to Sand Road Bridge: it is a mess, as can be seen from the put-in at Sand Road Bridge.

For either run, paddlers should recognize that Paradise Lake is on private property and should ask permission at the campground to put in or portage at the lake.

Campgrounds.
Atsion Lake Camp
Batona Camp
Bel Haven Lake
Buttonwood Camp
Goshen Pond Camp
Paradise Lake Campground

Canoe rental agencies.
Adams Canoe Rentals
Bel Haven Lake
Forks Landing Marina
Mullica River Boat Basin
Paradise Lake Campground

Public transportation. From New York City, one may travel by Atlantic City Coachways by purchasing a ticket to Hammonton. Upon arrival in the late afternoon, two options are available: 1) Ask the driver to stop at Lake Atsion, where canoes and hauling can be arranged (in advance) with Adams Canoe Rentals. Then, one can either put in at the Sand Road Bridge and paddle to Paradise Lake for camping, or go straight to Paradise Lake. Or 2) ask the driver to stop at the entrance road to Paradise Lake, a short distance beyond Lake Atsion, and walk about 1½ miles to the camp, where canoes can be rented. Possibly the walk can be avoided by making arrangements with Paradise Lake Campground to be picked up on the highway.

From Philadelphia the New Jersey Transit bus goes to Mount Holly. Walk to High Street and up High to Rancocas Road (about 2 blocks altogether) to catch the Atlantic City Coachways bus from New York City.

Other amenities. The nearest hospitals are in Hammonton and Mount Holly. Both cities have other amenities as well. Cabins are available for rent at Atsion Lake Camp. There are motels and diners on Route 206 north of Route 70 and a market on Route 206 south of Route 70.

Water level. The Braleys found the water to be 19 inches below the bridge on Route 206 and 36 inches below the concrete crosspiece above the spillway at Paradise Lake. The water level at the bridge behind the Pleasant Mills take-out is another good indicator of the water level in the Nescochague. Also, the owner of Paradise Lake Campground is familiar with the creek and is probably the best judge of current water conditions.

River details from Sand Road Bridge to Pleasant Mills. Albertson Brook has a moderate current and an initial width of about 1½ canoe lengths. On the left is a lovely stand of tall cedars; on the right are deciduous trees. In about ten minutes

138

there is a concrete structure, possibly from an old bridge or water gate, and the stream leaves the deep woods. A few minutes later the river passes through the remains of an old wooden bridge; a house lies back in the woods. Next, there is a concrete water-control culvert into the upper part of Paradise Lake; a canoe will just fit through the culvert. Soon campsites, a beach area, a dock, a canoe launch and buildings of Paradise Lake Campground appear on the south shore. From the Paradise Lake beach to the dam at the east end of the lake is about 500 yards.

The portage at the dam is on the right, along a path to a small, sandy, root-laced ledge just below the dam. Here, the water is dark amber, and the creek is about 1½ canoe lengths wide. The banks are lined with deciduous and cedar trees and are mostly free of overhanging bushes. The forest is dense, cool and dark, with little underbrush. Soon the river makes several turns and narrows to a width between ½ and 1 boat length, as it carves through the cedars. Some turns are sharp and require skill to maneuver the boat. Although the river is maintained, paddlers should be prepared to encounter new blowdowns.

Much of the river passes through lovely cedar swamps with tall trees. This portion is reputed to be a virgin cedar forest. In about thirty minutes, beaver lodges can be seen. In another twenty minutes, the river divides. The correct channel is on the right; the false channel on the left soon disappears into the woods. Debris is heavy here, and the best route is the one marked by cut logs. Through this area, the path is barely wide enough for the canoe and requires skill to get through. The water that follows the false channel trickles back through the debris, and the river widens again to 1½ canoe lengths. By this time Great Swamp Branch has joined from the right to form the Nescochague, but with so much debris a paddler is hard put to locate the actual confluence.

139

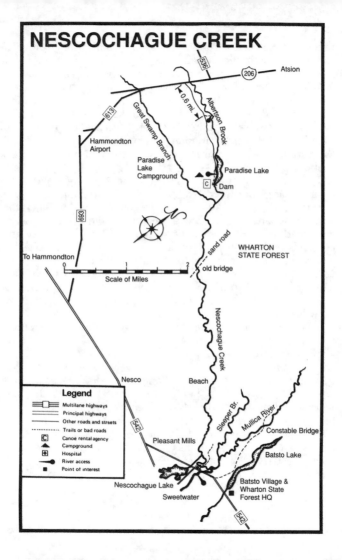

NESCOCHAGUE CREEK

536 206 Atsion

613

Great Swamp Branch

0.6 mi.

Albertson Brook

Hammondton Airport

Paradise Lake Campground

Paradise Lake

C Dam

699

sand road

WHARTON STATE FOREST

To Hammondton

0 1 2

Scale of Miles

old bridge

Nescochague Creek

Nesco

Beach

Sleeper Br.

Mullica River

Constable Bridge

542

Pleasant Mills

Batsto Lake

Nescochague Lake

Batsto Village & Wharton State Forest HQ

Sweetwater

542

Legend
- Multilane highways
- Principal highways
- Other roads and streets
- Trails or bad roads
- C Canoe rental agency
- ▲ Campground
- + Hospital
- River access
- ■ Point of interest

Nescochague Creek		Fraction Completed	
Access Points	Landmarks	Old bridge to Pleasant Mills	Paradise Lk. Camp to Pleasant Mills
Old Steel Bridge		0	
Paradise Lake Campground			0
	Dam	1/5	
	Sand Road bridge	1/2	2/5
	Campground	2/3	3/5
	Church bridge Mullica R.	9/10	9/10
Pleasant Mills	Route 542	1	1
River Rating		B	B
Canoeing Time, hrs.		3.5–4.5	3–4

In another fifteen minutes, there is a sandy beach on the left, one of the very few stopping places on this creek. Thirty feet away from the creek are a clearing and a sand road where wild blueberries grow, and a snack can easily be gathered during berry season. Moments after leaving this area, the river passes under a very old timber bridge. According to a ranger, it is the Jim George Bridge. The right bank of the river is not part of the state forest here.

The river continues its busy, twisted path through a deciduous forest. After about forty minutes, the debris and trees in the water become more dense, thanks largely to energetic beavers, and careful navigation is required to get through. Following an old burnt-over area, the forest opens to a beach on the right. Quickly the woods close in, and for the next hour one paddles through the dense forest, with little debris except for an occasional log to negotiate.

After about an hour of easy paddling, during which the out-flow of Nescochague Lake can be seen joining the creek from the right, the canoe arrives at the bridge behind the Pleasant Mills Church. Here the current is quite rapid, and the canoe must be maneuvered through debris trapped by the bridge. Within ten minutes, one comes into the Mullica River after ducking under a large tree. In a few minutes more the Route 542 bridge appears, and the Pleasant Mills canoe access is just downstream on the left.

16

Toms River

Outside the Wharton State Forest, the Toms River is probably the most popular river in the Pine Barrens. One reason is the proximity to the New York–New Jersey metropolitan area and the intensive development around the town of Toms River. Another is the length of the navigable part of the river, which is the second longest such run in the Pinelands. A third reason is its variety, from a narrow stream strewn with debris to a wide, clear flow into a tidal basin. One can paddle into the center of the town of Toms River. On the negative side, the Toms has more poison ivy than any other river in the Pine Barrens, and one of its access points remains one of the filthiest in the region.

Always an interesting river and a challenge for canoeists at any level of skill, the Toms has become even more so in recent years because the upper section is no longer well maintained. In this portion the headwaters of the Toms flow through a deciduous forest in tight, sharply twisted meanders with moderate to heavy patches of debris. The middle section, beginning at Whitesville, also contains debris but is more manageable, and the river passes beautiful stands of holly. The lower part is straighter and more piney.

During the Revolution the town of Toms River was a center for privateering, and a salt warehouse was located there. A windmill once stood in the middle of the river, near the town. Aside from that the river itself does not seem to have been prominent in our history. Of three possible sources for its name, the most favored is that it was named after a Thomas Luker who settled among the Indians on the river around 1700. Formerly, it was called Goose Creek.

Possible routes. Several roads cross the river, but for a number of reasons, access is limited. Traditionally, canoes were often put in on Route 528 in Cassville, but new guardrails were installed, preventing off-road parking. Currently the only nearby parking is a small community park about ¼ mile east of the bridge; from there, canoes would have to be portaged back to the bridge. The most convenient upper access is at Don Connor Boulevard. Don Connor Boulevard is shown as Coventry Road on old maps. It is still Coventry Road to some local people, so canoeists should know both road names in case they need directions.

The access at Bowman Road is also good. One advantage of the run from Bowman Road to Whitesville is the short shuttle, about 3 miles. People with only one car can walk from one end to the other in about an hour, but the river meanders so much that a rather full day is required to paddle it, particularly in its present condition. From Bowman Road to Whitesville may take as long as the trip from Whitesville to town.

Owing to the accumulation of debris that exists now, most people would not want to paddle the Toms River above Whitesville. In partial compensation, a new park, Winding River Park, runs along the left bank of the river from a point north of Route 527 for several miles to Route 37. In the park, the river is wilder and more attractive than in former days and includes a bike path and several picnic and rest spots. From Whitesville down, the best river accesses are at Whitesville, Winding River Park, and the town. Access at other crossings is

144

either difficult (owing to heavy traffic) or prohibited. The run from Whitesville to Toms River is best done in two days, but it can be done in one with an early start.

Campgrounds.
Albocondo Camp Grounds
Cedar Creek Camp Ground
Surf and Stream KOA Camp Site
Riverwood Park (open to Dover Township nonresidents if a permit is obtained in advance and in person)

Additionally, there are unposted areas along the river where it may be possible to stop for the night. I do not know whether camping is generally permitted at any of these spots, but it may be condoned if campers leave the sites unlittered and undisturbed. No one should start an open fire, anywhere, without a permit.

Canoe rental agencies.
Albocondo Camp Grounds
Art's Canoe Rentals (Cedar Creek Campground)
Pineland Canoes
Surf and Stream Canoe Rental

Public transportation. New Jersey Transit provides service from New York City to Lakewood and to Toms River, and from Philadelphia to Lakewood. By advance arrangement Pineland Canoes will pick up canoeists at either Lakewood or Toms River and transport them to the river.

Other amenities. Toms River has a shopping center on Route 37 just east of the Garden State Parkway. Routes 9 and 70 have several facilities. There is a hospital in Toms River, and a larger one in Lakewood.

Water level. For my runs, the water at Bowman Road was 57 inches below the bridge in the spring and 64 inches in the fall. On both trips the level of the river was about average. A gauge is now installed at the river access at Whitesville, on the upstream center piling of the bridge. A water level of 4.00 feet on this gauge corresponds to medium low; at this reading, the Braleys found the water was about 44 inches below the bridge at Don Connor Boulevard and 80 inches at Bowman Road. Even at this level, however, liftovers downstream are rare, and paddling downstream from Whitesville is usually reasonable. Above Whitesville the Toms can be paddled at this level but less water could compound the debris problem.

River details from Route 528 to Toms River. Throughout most of the upper section, the width of the Toms is usually 1 canoe length but sometimes slightly wider, and its meanderings are sharp, with frequent hairpin turns. The banks are of low to medium height and are covered thickly with grasses and deciduous bushes that often hang over the water and obstruct passage. The trees, also deciduous, are large and thinly spaced but gradually become crowded and more slender. Brier hangs from the trees in great sheets or dangles from bushes, which can cause entanglement for a canoe. Holly appears occasionally on the banks and, when the leaves are gone, contrasts with the bareness of the surroundings. Moderate to heavy amounts of debris are encountered, much of it requiring liftovers. The river continues for some time in the same vein: debris to work through or around, with liftovers; moderate to thickly packed trees; dense bushes and brier along the banks; and frequent sharp turns.

A short time later the river passes through the right-of-way of a high-voltage power line where the dense growth has been cleared and replaced by grasses. The stream meanders wildly for several minutes in the open field before drawing alongside

146

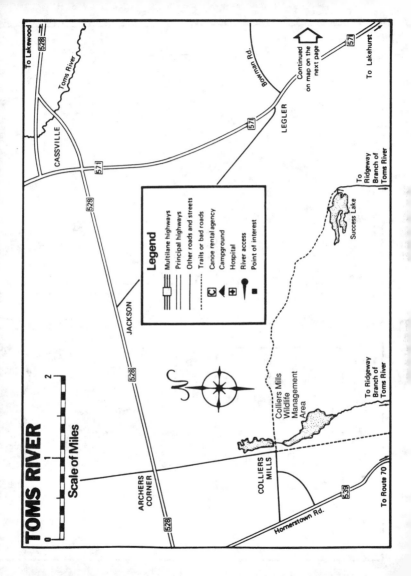

TOMS RIVER

Scale of Miles

0 1 2

Legend

Multilane highways
Principal highways
Other roads and streets
Trails or bad roads
Canoe rental agency
Campground
Hospital
River access
Point of interest

To Lakewood

Toms River

CASSVILLE

528

57

57j

LEGLER

Bowman Rd.

Continued on map on the next page

57

To Lakehurst

JACKSON

528

ARCHERS CORNER

528

COLLIERS MILLS

Hornerstown Rd.

539

To Route 70

Colliers Mills Wildlife Management Area

To Ridgeway Branch of Toms River

Success Lake

To Ridgeway Branch of Toms River

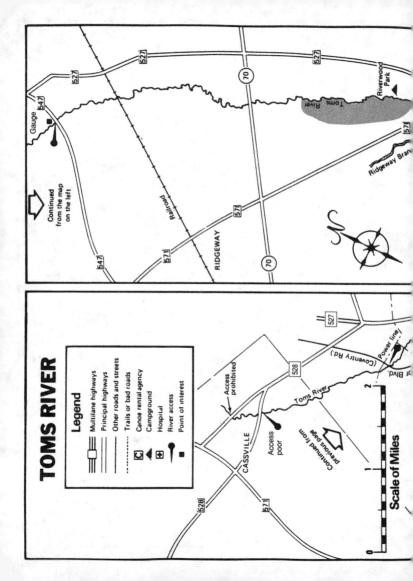

TOMS RIVER

Legend

≡ Multilane highways
— Principal highways
— Other roads and streets
⋯ Trails or bad roads
◧ Canoe rental agency
▲ Campground
⊞ Hospital
● River access
■ Point of interest

Access prohibited

CASSVILLE

Access poor

Toms River

(Coventry Rd.)

Power line

or Blvd.

Scale of Miles

0   1   2

Continued from previous page

Gauge

Continued from the map on the left

Toms River

Riverwood Park

RIDGEWAY

Ridgeway Branch

Railroad

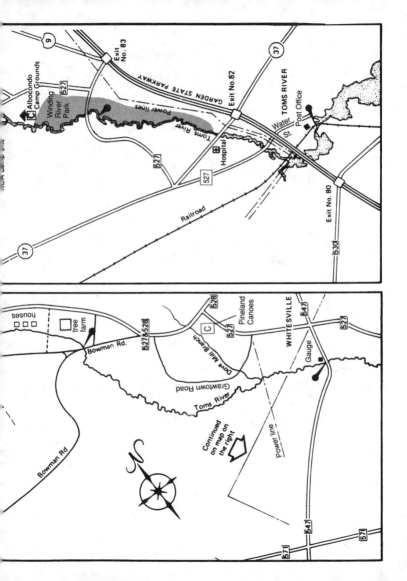

Toms River		Fraction Completed		
Access Points	Landmarks	Route 528 to Toms River	Route 528 to Bowman Road	Don Connor Blvd. to Whitesville
Route 528	Cassville	0	0	
	Enter powerline area		1/2	
Don Connor Blvd. Road				0
	Power line		3/4	1/10
Bowman Road		1/3	1	1/3
	Canal			1/2
	Power line			4/5
Route 547	Whitesville	2/3		1
Route 70				
	Riverwood Park, 1st campsite			
Route 571				
	Route 527			
Winding River Park		9/10		
	Bike path			
	Route 37 Route 527 GS Parkway			
Toms River Post Office	Parking lot	1		
River Rating		C+	C	C−
Canoeing Time, hrs.		Several days	3.5–5.5	6.5–8

150

Fraction Completed			
Bowman Road to Whitesville	Whitesville to Toms River	Whitesville to Route 571	Route 571 to Toms River
0			
1/3			
3/4			
1	0	0	
	1/3	1/2	
		3/4	
	1/2	1	0
	2/3		1/4
			2/3
	1		1
C	B	A	A
4.5–6	4.5–6	2.5–3.5	2–2.5

151

a dry, sandy bank that is good for a rest stop. Then the river turns into the woods and passes under the bridge at Don Connor Boulevard.

Debris gradually becomes heavier again. Bushes and brier hang over the water, but the trees are more thinly spaced than before, giving a more open appearance to the river. Turns continue to be very sharp and frequent. Eventually, a cleared area on the left offers a possible rest stop, which is soon followed by a low-voltage power line.

Turns become less frequent. A tributary enters on the left, and the adjacent grassy spot makes a good rest stop. The river passage is clearer, and there are few overhanging bushes. Occasionally one sees a thin stand of cedars and pines, or a holly tree. Soon the turns become sharp and frequent again, but only for a few minutes. Houses appear on the left, and then the river passes under a sand road that is part of a tree farm operated by the state Forestry Department. A short walk up a path on the left leads to seed-tree orchards of several species. Trout are also stocked here, according to some local fly fishermen, Trout Unlimited (an organization of sports fishermen) may try to establish a permanent trout habitat. Downstream from the road there are several sharp turns that may be clogged with debris. A short time later, one passes under the Bowman Road bridge.

After five to ten minutes of frequent meanders, a low cleared spot appears on the left; a wide trail there leads to a large field of pines. The river's turns soon become gentle and infrequent. An occasional tree lies in the water. This is the first area in which poison ivy is obvious; it grows on the trees and debris projecting over the river. Sometimes, while squeezing under a log, one must contort oneself more than usual in order to avoid the poison ivy that dangles there.

The type of foliage begins to change—hummocks of grasses become more common and trees more scattered. The scenery takes on an open aspect. The banks become more swampy and the river meanders, sometimes in sharp hairpin turns, through grassy fields with some low bushes and occasional, isolated trees. Some of the very tall trees are dead, and vines hang from their branches. Poison ivy is common near the water. Brier is also common, sometimes in dead, matted patches. Looking to the side through the grass, one can often see another part of the river flowing in the opposite direction.

Soon the Toms passes back into woods. The foliage closes in, with overhanging bushes and brier, and becomes very dense. Debris occurs frequently. After a time a canal appears straight ahead. The river, however, turns sharply left in the first of many hairpin turns. The banks are swampy. The water spreads out, passing through bushes and sometimes forming more than one channel. Usually it is best to stay where the water flow is heaviest unless there is an obvious shortcut through the bushes. Somewhere in the midst of this swamp a high-voltage power line crosses overhead.

The river continues to wind through swampy bushes. Care must be taken to follow the channel. Poison ivy makes spectacular displays by sending its stems up from dead stumps in the water. One such stand resembles a curled finger or figure 9. Debris and liftovers are frequent. The swamp continues in this way for some time. Eventually it becomes better defined, and soon the Doves Mill Branch enters on the left. The turns are still sharp and frequent, with the customary debris. But soon the banks become firmer and the bushes thinner. A few minutes later one arrives at the bridge at Whitesville.

The access at Whitesville is easily recognized at most times by the accumulation of litter, although it is cleaned up occasionally. Considerable development is occurring in this area, and the riverbanks downstream of the bridge for about 50 feet have been cleared for a pipeline or sewer crossing.

Below Whitesville several trees, some of them large, lean

precipitously over the water; the soil has eroded from around their roots. Other trees stand in the river on small clumps of soil which their roots hold in place. Mosses, lichens and poison ivy grow on the trees. Within ten minutes one comes to a stopping place on the left where a sandy trail leads to an open field. Then the river passes under a railroad trestle and to a pumping station on the right. Patches of pines appear occasionally along the higher banks; sheep laurel appears often on the slopes. On the right a flat pine area cleared of underbrush offers a good stopping place.

For the first time, many holly trees can be seen. The meanders of the river are inconsistent. Debris is considerably less severe, although an occasional liftover may be necessary in low water. After some time, one comes to a spot where both banks are cleared; perhaps there used to be a bridge here. On the right there is a house set well back from the bank, but a low ramp on the left makes a good stopping place. About five minutes later, one passes under Route 70.

The river borders a mobile home development for a few minutes and then turns and parallels a quarry on the right, which is mostly hidden behind bushes on high ground. The river widens to 1½ or 2 canoe lengths, with gentle and infrequent turns. Holly is still common. A pump station appears on the right; rigging from the station leads to the quarry. In ten or fifteen minutes there is a campsite on the left, the first of three in Riverwood Park. (The other two appear within the next ten or fifteen minutes.) The low-lying shore of the park is covered with trees, and stone benches line a footpath along the water near the far end. The river turns frequently through here. Following the park there is an extensive and obtrusive housing development on the right. A few minutes past it, the river passes under Route 571.

The river continues turning frequently for several minutes, and there is considerable debris in the water. The Union

Branch then enters from the right, widening the stream to 2 canoe lengths; at this point, there are few turns and little debris. Albocondo Camp Grounds can soon be seen on the left, although a hairpin meander must be negotiated before arriving there. A short time later, the posted property of the Toms River Plant of the Ciba-Geigy Corporation appears on the right. The banks become medium to high, sandy and covered with scattered pines and low bushes. The growth is rather dry looking in comparison with the lush bushes upstream. Some cranberries can be seen. A power station soon appears on the right, and in a few minutes the river meanders back and forth next to a wire fence. At one time this was an unpleasant section, when odors from the chemical plant hovered over the water for a fifteen- to twenty-minute stretch. The plant has often been accused of committing pollution violations and spilling waste into the river; perhaps the publicity has had an effect, because lately the aroma has not been noticeable.

The river widens further to about 3 canoe lengths. Several minutes later the canoe passes under Route 527. In another few minutes an open, sandy area appears on the left. This is the canoe access area for Winding River Park.

The banks gradually become lower and are occasionally swampy. The trees and bushes take on a more deciduous appearance. In about twenty minutes, a bridge crosses the river. The bridge is for the bikepath through the park, and it parallels the river on the right for the next 2 miles or so. Several good stopping points are available along this stretch. The river meanders constantly. After some time it makes a hairpin turn around a very good, sandy beach where a rope hangs high over the outside of the bend. Pilings crossing the river here are all that remains of a wooden bridge. Pine trees disappear, and in a short time the river runs under Route 37.

At this point the Toms River becomes tidal. It turns left toward the cleared and marshy right-of-way of a high-voltage power line. Then it turns away from it and meanders tightly back and forth. After crossing under Route 527 for the second time, the river turns left and meanders across the right-of-way three times. Passing under a low-voltage power line, it turns right through thin woods near buildings that are the outskirts of the town of Toms River. It passes under a railroad trestle and a gas pipeline and leaves the woods, losing its identity in a broad marsh. One should then turn left and paddle under the Garden State Parkway, keeping close to the bushes on the left. There is a channel here; it swings left before a bush-covered island and then right around a lumberyard. Then it crosses under the railroad trestle again; on the other side is the public boat ramp at the back of the commuter parking lot behind the Toms River post office. At high tide, a canoe may not be able to pass under this trestle, in which case the canoe may be taken out here and carried to the parking lot.

17

~~~~~~

Cedar Creek

Cedar Creek may be a new river for many canoeists, although the lower section is becoming increasingly popular. The lower section is broad and ranks with the Pine Barrens' easier streams, but the upper section is narrow, often shallow, sharply twisting and filled with small islands. The river is swampy through most of its length.

Except near the lower end, the river is not closed in like the Batsto and Oswego. The cedars that must have lined its banks many years ago are now thinly interspersed with bushes and marsh grasses. The water is probably the clearest and least colored in the Pine Barrens. When it is deep, perhaps 6 to 8 feet, one can still see to the bottom, much of which is covered by gracefully bending underwater grasses.

Much of the canoeable portion of Cedar Creek is within Double Trouble State Park. The park is named after a village on the river where a dam, cranberry bog and ruins of a sawmill are located. The wooden dam was constructed to power the sawmill. As the story goes, the dam washed out, and a worker said, "Here's trouble." We can guess what he said (along with other unprintable remarks) when it washed out a second time. The state originally purchased this small area, leased it for cranberry growing, and set up an interpretive center open to anyone wishing to learn how cranberries are raised and harvested. After a time it was vandalized. Then the land was reassessed upward, and the cranberry grower was driven out of business. Upstream is another cranberry field that was owned and used as a camp by the Ocean County Girl Scout Council. It too was vandalized, abandoned and eventually sold to the state.

The water in Cedar Creek is considered among the purest in the Pine Barrens, but the area has been subjected to the effects of development. At one time, local residents successfully opposed the construction of a waste treatment plant on the banks. Portions upstream were owned by developers and were zoned for industrial use. A local group, the Citizens' Conservation Council of Ocean County, struggled for the preservation of the stream, and we are beneficiaries of their success. Unfortunately, much of the beauty and purity of the river, especially downstream from the old Girl Scout camp, is being threatened by the litter that accompanies increased use of any river.

Headquarters for the park are in the village of Double Trouble. Most of the work being done at the park is in planning for development of the site. An archeological study of the sawmill is being carried out, preceding its restoration. An old cottage belonging to one of the cranberry pickers is being converted to restrooms and office facilities. For canoeists, a new and more convenient canoe access is being constructed to replace the old put-in at Dover Forge. Also, a self-guided nature trail, including a tour and description of the local cranberry fields, has been set up in the village and offers a pleasant diversion for canoeists.

At one time Cedar Creek had two iron furnaces—one at Bamber Lake, called Ferrago Forge, and the other at Dover Forge.

Possible routes. Cedar Creek is navigable from Bamber to Lanoka Harbor. Above Lacey Road it is clogged with debris.

158

The whole run can be made in one rather long day, but the river is normally paddled in shorter sections. Good accesses are available at Dover Forge, Double Trouble and Western Boulevard. Access is also available at the old Girl Scout camp, but it is inferior to the others and is heavily used by liveries; anyone leaving a car there should park well off to the side, to avoid heavy canoe trailer traffic down to the river. From Lacey Road to Dover Forge is narrow, shallow and swampy, and it should be run only by experienced canoeists. Don't be fooled by the appearance of the river at Lacey Road, because it narrows down within ten minutes.

Parking is forbidden on Route 9. If a take-out is planned there, one should park on a side road.

Campgrounds.
Albocondo Camp Grounds
Cedar Creek Camp Ground
Surf and Stream KOA Camp Site

Canoe rental agencies.
Art's Canoe Rentals
Triple T Canoe Livery

Somewhat more remote are:
Albocondo Camp Grounds
Pineland Canoes
Surf and Stream Canoe Rental

Public transportation. New Jersey Transit provides service from New York City to Bayville, where one can rent canoes at Cedar Creek Camp Ground and arrange for hauling. Ask the bus driver to stop at the entrance to Cedar Creek Camp Ground; from there the walk to the camp office is about 500 feet. When returning, the bus can be flagged down across the highway from the camp.

To get to Bayville from Philadelphia, one may take the New Jersey Transit bus to Lakewood and transfer to the bus from New York City.

Other amenities. Toms River has a shopping center on Route 37 just east of the Garden State Parkway. Routes 9 and 70 have several facilities. There is also a market on Dover Road, just west of the Garden State Parkway. There is a hospital in Toms River, and a larger one in Lakewood.

Water level. During my trips, the water at Lacey Road was 52 inches below the bridge in the spring and 55 inches in the fall. These are the levels under normal conditions. A gauge is now installed on the upstream side of the Lacey Road bridge, attached to the east abutment (river right). A reading of 52 inches would be about 4.06 feet on the gauge. The Braleys paddled at readings of 3.40 and 4.56 feet and found enough water at the lower reading. Scraping the bottom is likely only in the upper section from Lacey Road to Dover Forge.

River details from Lacey Road to Lanoka Harbor. The river at Lacey Road is reasonably wide at the beginning, about 1 to 1½ canoe lengths. The banks are low and often swamped in high water. The trees are deciduous, with scattered cedars. Thick deciduous bushes often overhang the river, narrowing the passageway. Some bushes grow out of the water, and there are rushes in the swampy areas. The current is moderate to strong. The turns are usually gentle as long as the river remains wide. A moderate amount of debris in the water further constricts the route, although few liftovers are necessary, except perhaps in low water.

The water is clear. Against the white sand on the river bottom, it seems to be colored a light tan. Thick patches of underwater grass (mostly pipewort) cling to the bottom with their blades drifting downstream, looking like green boulders beneath the surface.

Within ten minutes after the put-in, the river narrows considerably to 1 or 2 canoe widths. In high water the river spreads out and flows around and through numerous islands, but the effect is still the same: a constriction of the main channel. A house on a sandy beach comes into view; it is the only one on the river. There is a good stand of pines at the beach, and cedars become more common.

From here to Dover Forge, the channel width fluctuates between ½ canoe width and 1 canoe length as it is constricted by islands. They vary from 2 to 12 feet across and are heavily covered with bushes, cedars and moss. Turns are sharp and frequent around the islands and cedar debris. The cedar trees grow quite thick, though not as tall as on the Batsto or Oswego rivers, so the view is more open. When not predominant, cedars are mixed with maples. Occasionally, there is a swamp magnolia along the bank. The river continues this way to the new canoe access at Dover Forge, on the left.

Soon the water begins to widen into a swamp. It may be shallow and require careful maneuvering around the underwater grasses and logs. Cedars are less frequent. The river becomes very wide, and a large patch of dead trees stands on the left shore. At the pond, trees are replaced by a field of grasses and low shrubbery through which the river, about 3 canoe lengths wide, gently meanders. Pines can be seen on the distant banks. At the foot of the pond, where a dam was once located to provide power for the forge, the water drops gently into a pool. The pool and bordering bank are good for lunch and a swim.

Below the pond the river narrows to ½ or 1 canoe length; the current is swift, initially with gentle turns. Dense bushes

161

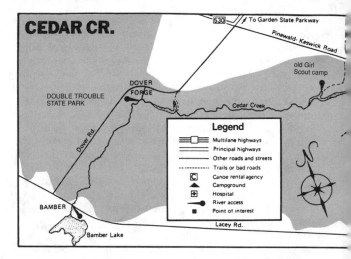

and cedars line the banks. After several minutes the trees thin out, and cedars are replaced by scattered maples. Soon there may be some debris to push through, but elsewhere it is not usually significant. The river widens to 1 to 1½ canoe lengths and meanders rather sharply. There is little underwater grass; wood and sand on the bottom can be seen clearly through the yellowish tan water. The growth of maple trees is often dense. Mixed bushes and marsh grasses remain crowded along the shore. Beaver are in evidence here and the canoe may have to be pushed over a beaver dam.

The trees become scattered again and the river opens up; along the banks grow mostly bushes and grasses. On a sunny day one can see shadows from ripples made by the canoe playing along the sandy bottom. The turns are gentle and infrequent, except when the river passes by the small bush-covered islands that are beginning to appear. Firm, bushy

162

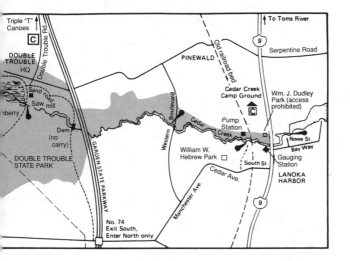

banks alternate with swamp foliage. Underwater grasses tint the river a light yellow-green. For several minutes the river widens to 3 canoe lengths and the deepest section meanders from one bank to the other through protruding grasses. Then it narrows, more islands pass by and cedars reappear, gradually becoming common. Debris occurs frequently. Soon a canal appears on the left leading to an abandoned cranberry field. This is the site of the old Girl Scout camp.

Depending on the water level, the river may narrow for several minutes or only briefly, but sooner or later it widens to 2 or 3 canoe lengths and passes around small islands. Dense stands of cedars grow along the banks. Underwater grasses are profuse. Several islands later, all trees disappear as the river crosses under a high-voltage power line. Then it spreads out and becomes a pond filled with dead wood and many stumps, created by the first of three dams at Double Trouble. This is

Cedar Creek		Fraction Completed				
Access Points	Landmarks	Bamber to Lanoka Harbor	Bamber to Old Girl Scout Camp	Dover Forge to Railroad Trestle	Old Girl Scout Camp to Railroad Trestle	Double Trouble HQ to Western Blvd.
Lacey Rd., Bamber		0	0			
Dover Forge		1/4	3/5	0		
Old Girl Scout Camp			1	1/3	0	
	Power line	1/2				
	Carry Dam			2/5	1/5	
Double Trouble St. Forest HQ	Sawmill	2/3			2/5	0
	Dam	7/10		2/3		1/3
	GS Parkway					
Western Blvd.		4/5			4/5	1
Railroad Trestle	Dudley Pk.	9/10		1	1	
Lanoka Harbor	Route 9 Spillway	1				
River Rating		B –	B	B	A	A
Canoeing Time, hrs.		5.5–8	3–4	4–5	3–4	1.5–2

164

not a pleasant place and headwinds can make the crossing slow, but it is short. At the end is the first dam; it is partially rebuilt and requires a portage. Canoes should be carried over on the right by following a concrete road ford and flood spillway for about 50 feet.

At one time the first and second dams controlled the water flow into the main cranberry field at Double Trouble, and a paddler did not know in advance whether he or she would be floating on a pond or a stream. Now, however, the second dam is gone, and the river channel meanders gently through the cranberry bushes, dense underbrush and small trees of the recovering forest. A few old pilings indicate the former presence of footbridges. A white bridge shows the location of what was once the second dam. This is the village of Double Trouble, now the headquarters of the state park. Cars may be driven to the bridge to leave canoes, but they must be parked at the headquarters. The walk from the bridge to the parking area takes about six minutes. A descriptive guide to the nature trail can be obtained at the old packing shed.

From this point the river is clear of debris, except for occasional trees and brush felled by beaver. On both sides are cranberry bogs, but they cannot be seen through the foliage along the banks. The river narrows to 1 canoe length. The banks are low and covered with bushes, particularly cranberry along the edge, and trees arch overhead. The river widens to 2 canoe lengths and meanders sharply several times. In about ten minutes, it crosses under a footbridge that has a log rest bench in the center. The bridge is part of the nature trail through the cranberry bogs.

Then the river opens into a broad marsh containing a variety of plants: grasses, cranberries, small cedars, leatherleaf, maples and water lilies, all contributing to a range of delicate colors in both spring and fall. The current is almost nil, so one should be wary of false channels. The most direct route is to

166

paddle straight ahead to the end, bear left and continue straight to the third dam. No portage is required. The original floodgate is now the New Guinea Bridge, which has a sign noting that stairs are on the far side. By climbing the stairs, one can look back to the marsh and the cranberry bogs in Double Trouble.

The river is now 1 or 1½ canoe lengths wide with few turns. Bushes and some trees line the banks. After a few minutes it passes under the Garden State Parkway. The foliage becomes dense, although the widened channel gives an impression of openness. There are several gentle meanders. The water, less clear now, is like the darker streams elsewhere. Tall stands of cedar appear again, and at one point, about twenty minutes past the Garden State Parkway, there is a beautiful mixture of cedars and swamp magnolias on the left. Sometimes the turns are sharp for a short distance. The banks are low and often swampy or washed out. The current is usually sluggish. Forty or fifty minutes after the third dam, the river makes a sharp hairpin turn around a low, sandy island. Although very cool in the shadow of the cedars, it is a pleasant spot for a rest. Around the next bend there is a small landing on the left that is also good for a stop. Just beyond is Western Boulevard.

This is a popular access for a take-out, with parking about 100 feet from the river. There is an extensive soft sand beach, and it is a frequent swimming and drinking spot for local people. The pile of litter confirms its popularity.

Fluctuating in size, the river gradually widens from 1½ to 2 canoe lengths. The shore seems drier with the appearance of evergreen bushes. Debris from beaver activity may be prominent about ten minutes from Western Boulevard. A beaver lodge can be seen on the left, with a dam under construction. The channel meanders, usually amiably, for some time; eventually, the river takes a sharp horseshoe bend, beyond which is a railroad trestle. At the present time, this is the last satisfactory take-out for most people. (Access at William J. Dudley Park at Route 9 is restricted to Berkeley Township residents, and the gate may be chained and the park closed except for the summer season.) Most paddlers should take out above the trestle on the hard-packed sand area in the horseshoe bend, on the right, but those renting from Cedar Creek Campground should take out below the trestle on the left, at a private road on campground property. Those who continue beyond the trestle must go down the center because both sides are blocked with rocks and old pilings from previous bridges.

18

~~~~~~

Oyster Creek

While canoeing the Toms River and Cedar Creek, I met two people who knew Oyster Creek and thought it would make a good canoe trip. Later, when scouting it by car, I found that the put-in looked so attractive as to be irresistible, On the other hand, the river is short and passes by the nuclear power station of the New Jersey Central Power and Light Company on Route 9. I was unable to find a canoe club that had tried the river, so I ran it on a cold, clear late-fall day.

The results were mixed. Oyster Creek, whose name came from the many shellfish once harvested from its bottom, is a beautiful river. It runs through an open bog with young cedars growing along the banks. There is scarcely any debris except at the end, where trees that were cleared from the land around the power station were pushed into the stream. There the river is a mess for about 100 yards. Perhaps it can be run in higher water; perhaps it may be cleared by natural causes or some person's hard work; or perhaps the agency responsible can be forced to remove the rubble. In addition, a sandy area about thirty minutes downstream from Route 532 appears to be occupied regularly by off-road vehicle enthusiasts who are tossing their worn-out tires into the creek. These are examples of how an attractive and useful river can be vandalized. Even so, Oyster Creek is enjoyable on a warm day if one does not object to wading, scrambling among logs or maneuvering around tires in the water.

Since the cooling water passing through the canal of the power station is shielded from the atomic generator, it is not considered radioactive. Its warmth has attracted numerous fish to the area, and the mouth of the canal is a favorite fishing ground. Unfortunately, many of the fish are killed when the power station shuts down and the water turns cold.

Possible routes. Oyster Creek can be run from Wells Mills Park to Route 9, with access at Route 532 for either putting in or taking out. The park contains a parking area, access to the reservoir and access to the creek at a small wooden bridge 50 yards down a sand road east of the parking area. Canoes can be carried down the sand road, which can be negotiated only with a four-wheel-drive vehicle. The upper section, between Wells Mills Park and Route 532, is much more strenuous than the lower section, primarily owing to river debris; it should not be attempted without a bow saw and long-handled pruning clippers. Anyone trying to keep the river clear is fighting the owners of the adjoining land, who cut trees so that they fall across the river and serve as footbridges. On the other hand, the river downstream from Route 532 has customarily been cleared for fishing and is more open.

Campgrounds.
Cedar Creek Camp Ground
Lebanon State Forest

Canoe rental agency.
Cedar Creek Camp Ground (hauling service is unlikely)

Public transportation. None.

Other amenities. Route 9 has services. There are hospitals at Toms River and Lakewood.

Water level. In the fall when I ran Oyster Creek, the water was 44 inches below the bridge at Route 532. The river was deep most of the way, but underwater growth limited passage, so it would not be wise to run the river at a level much lower than 44 inches at the bridge.

The bridge at Route 532 is now a river gauge station, with three scales: one upstream of the spillway behind the gauge house, one under the bridge and the third downstream on the end of the abutment. When the Braleys ran the river downstream from Route 532, the readings were 4.70 feet on the upstream scale, 2.59 under the bridge and 3.85 downstream. The water was 42 inches below the bridge at Route 532 and about 34 inches below the bridge at Wells Mills Park. At Wells Mills the upstream section of the river did not appear to be navigable. On another day after a heavy rain, the water at Wells Mills Park rose to 26 inches, although gauge readings on Route 532 were within ½ inch of the previous readings. As it turned out, the gauge station was more reliable than measurements at Wells Mills Park.

River details from Wells Mills Park to Route 9. Below the wooden bridge near the eastern end of the reservoir, the river is very narrow, about 2 canoe widths. The channel winds among closely spaced cedar trees. Dead branches wedged among the trees create blockages, which are, however, easy to negotiate. In about a half hour a pine-covered bluff can be seen through dead cedars on the right. On this run the water in the channel was deep, but it spread out among the trees and so was probably higher than normal. Sometimes it was difficult to stay in the channel. Soon a pond is entered, and two houses can be seen on the left shore.

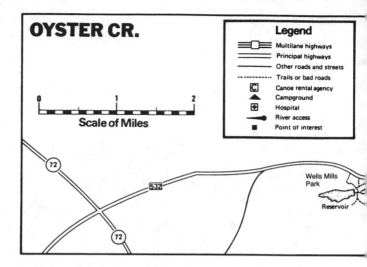

On the far side of the pond to the right of the houses is a sand road with a concrete culvert guarded by a semicircular dam. The canoe can be carried around the dam on the left, beyond which is a sand beach. The river becomes wider, lower and more open. It is attractive, with grasses growing in the water, but very shortly the first of three major blockages—a combination of blowdowns and crude, man-made bridges—is encountered. A canoe can be carried around it on the right. After passing through debris, some of which requires liftovers, the second logjam is approached, and the canoe must be carried around on the left. The canoe can be dragged over the third. Through here the river width is about ½ a canoe length, but the debris usually prevents anyone taking advantage of this.

Beyond the third logjam, the canoe must be threaded around downed cedars and through very narrow channels cre-

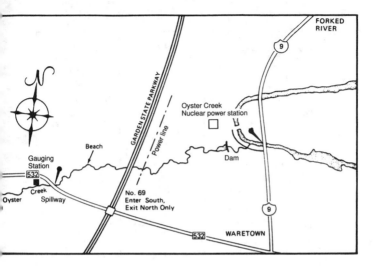

ated by small live cedars growing on hummocks. Following this challenge are the spillway and bridge at Route 532. The spillway provides a small swimming area above the bridge. At high water a canoe can scrape over the spillway; otherwise it should be lifted over or carried around the spillway. If water is very high, be sure there is enough room to pass under the bridge.

After the bridge, the river is still narrow—about 3 canoe widths—but the lack of debris allows one to relax a bit and enjoy the beauty. The water is clear and light colored, and the river bottom is densely covered with green grasses. Cedars of medium height line the banks. The river soon widens to 1 canoe length, and the turns are gentle. The current is strong at the beginning but becomes generally moderate. The banks become low and swampy. The cedars thin out where they grow among marsh grasses and sphagnum moss. Frequently,

173

Oyster Creek		Fraction Completed	
Access Points	Landmarks	Wells Mills Park to Route 9	Route 532 to Route 9
Wells Mills Park		0	
	Dam	1/6	
Route 532	Spillway	2/5	0
	Sandy bank	3/5	1/4
	Garden State Parkway	2/3	1/3
	Dam	8/10	7/10
Route 9		1	1
River Rating		C	B
Canoeing Time, Hrs.		4.5–5.	2.5–3

174

one can see beyond the river into an open field of grasses and cedar saplings. There is some debris in the water, usually deep under the surface. Underwater grasses, however, are dense and restrict passage through the narrow channel. A pitcher plant appears on a rare occasion. Some leatherleaf grows on the bank, and rushes grow in the water.

The cedars became patchy and then thinly scattered in the open, boggy field. Water depth may be as much as 4 feet, but underwater grasses block much of the passage. Wood seen underwater is often coated with dark, flowing moss. In a short while, a few deciduous bushes and trees begin to appear. A half-hour from the put-in, there is an open, sandy bank high on the left where the ruins of a cinder-block house are located. The site is littered with beer cans and tires. But there is also a fine swimming hole at this spot, from 4 to 6 feet deep, and on the right bank is a dense stand of evergreen bushes and trees.

Immediately downstream is a sequence of four wooden fish weirs. At the fall water level, all were easy liftovers. In higher water, fewer weirs may be seen, and they may not require liftovers. The banks are slightly higher, firmer and crowded with low bushes. The view continues to be open, and the bog is replaced by bushes. One can see cedars, some scrub maples and some pines. A few slender gray birches along the banks appear prominent because of their light bark. The river gradually widens to 1½ or 2 canoe lengths with gentle and infrequent turns. In a short time the river passes under the Garden State Parkway and then a power line. A resting spot near the power line contains considerable trash.

A few minutes later the river narrows to just 1 canoe length, and there is a brief, slow passage through a patch of considerable debris. Cedars are dense; tall stands of them grow along the banks, sometimes overhanging the river and shading it completely save for a few glints of sunlight on the underwater grasses and rushes. After a few minutes the trees thin out, and the view is open once again. Some lily pads appear. Trees become sparse and banks become very bushy. In another few minutes, a tributary enters on the left, and one can spot the power station soon after. The river meanders through an open, swampy field of thick, low bushes immersed in water.

The swamp ends as the river flows into a small pond just above the power station. At the lower end there is a dam, which is difficult to spot. The canoe must be portaged around the right side of a wooden retaining wall. Downstream there is an open, devastated area cleared of trees where only some field grass grows. The channel is choked with debris but is still passable. As the river turns into woods, however, one is confronted with a view of 100 yards or so of logs strewn about in the water. One should be careful to avoid slipping on these logs. A half-hour and numerous liftovers later, the debris ends at a utility road. Several large, round, corrugated metal tubes carry the river under the road, and a canoe can just pass through one of them and on into a canal that carries water swiftly from the power station. In a few minutes the railroad trestle next to Route 9 is reached.

19

Metedeconk River

Like most rivers in the Pine Barrens, the Metedeconk requires continual maintenance to be navigable. It is short and for the most part does not have the charm of other rivers, but it is more convenient to the heavily populated areas of New York and northern New Jersey. The first edition of this book described a run on the North Branch, from Brook Road to Forge Pond, because this had been cleared by a local group. Maintenance, however, apparently stopped just as the book came out, and now most of the North Branch is so choked up with debris that it is not worth running, despite the fact that it is free of poison ivy. Also, logs are often piled upon one another, and the likelihood of an accident is high, especially under slippery conditions. Debris is manageable and liftovers are few downstream from Route 549, and a short trip of about one to one and a half hours is possible.

In contrast, canoeing the South branch has been encouraged by the development of Lake Shenandoah County Park and Field Sports Complex, which includes a canoe launch area. It is still challenging and some liftovers are likely, but it is not dangerous. One disadvantage of the South Branch is that it runs parallel to Route 80; although businesses along the road cannot be seen through the brush, they can be heard. Accordingly, it is best canoed on a Sunday.

The upper part of Forge Pond and the run to the park at the take-out are very attractive and worth a trip on either branch. Considerable bird life is evident on the upper part; for example, herons and egrets can be seen in early summer.

There are three possible sources of the Metedeconk's name. The Maltikkongy Indians used to live in the region of the Delaware. The Indian word *mettig-conck* means "a place where there is good." And two other Indian words—*meteu* meaning "medicine man" and *saconk* meaning "outlet of stream"—may be a combined source. At any rate, today the river's name is pronounced "Me-tee'de-conk," with the accent on the second syllable.

Possible routes. A reasonable but short run on the North Branch is from Route 549 to Forge Pond. Access at Route 549, however, is limited and not as good as access at Route 88, where the old Route 88 pavement next to the new bridge provides excellent access. Those who insist on putting in at Brook Road "because it's there" are on their own as far as this edition is concerned. The bridge at Ridge Road is being rebuilt and may offer an alternate access in the future, but in any case, a saw and long-handled pruning clippers are absolutely necessary above Route 549. On the South Branch, the run from Lake Shenandoah Park to Forge Pond is longer than from Route 549 to Forge Pond on the North Branch, but it still can be run on a short day by most canoeists. Here again, long-handled clippers to trim vegetation may be helpful.

Campgrounds.
Albocondo Camp Grounds
Pine Cone Campground
Surf and Stream KOA Camp Site

178

Canoe rental agencies.
Albocondo Camp Grounds (hauling unlikely)
Pineland Canoes (hauling unlikely)
Walt's Sunoco Service (no hauling)

Public transportation. None.

Other amenities. Routes 9 and 70 have many services. There is a hospital in Lakewood.

Water level. For the North Branch, most of the data is for the water level at Brook Road, which is not only inconvenient but probably unreliable as an indicator for canoeing downstream from Route 549. One reading at high water was taken when the water was 46 inches below the bottom of the upstream side of the new bridge at Route 88. On the South Branch, a gauge is located at the bridge at Route 549, river left. (Note that Route 549 crosses both branches, so don't get mixed up.) A summer reading on this gauge was 5.0 feet. Perhaps the best estimate of water in the South Branch can be made by looking upstream from Route 549. There, a large tree can be seen blocking the river; at the present time it is the biggest obstacle on the South Branch.

River details for the North Branch from Route 549 to Forge Pond. The river is narrow, about 1 to 1½ canoe lengths. It contains some debris, which necessitates an occasional lift-over. Bushes and trees line the river, but not severely. In about twenty or twenty-five minutes, the river crosses under the Garden State Parkway, Route 88 and a low-voltage power line in quick succession. Then it diverges around an island; the channel on the right is the narrower, but by following it one avoids a liftover on the left. Gradually, the banks become lower, and the river occasionally overflows into a swamp.

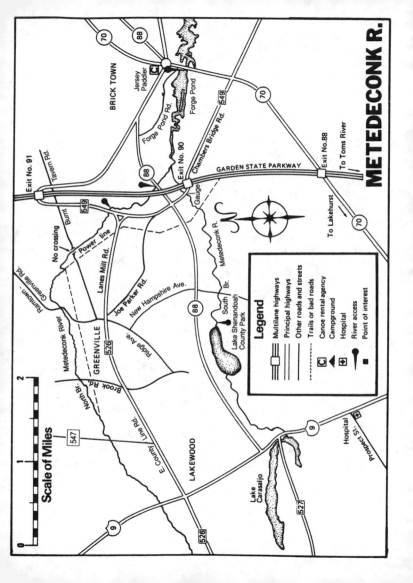

North Branch Metedeconk R.		Fraction Completed
Access Points	**Landmarks**	**Rte. 549 To Forge Pond**
Rte. 549	GS Pkway	0
Route 88	So. Branch	1/2
Forge Pond		1
River Rating		A
Canoeing Time, hrs.		1.5–2

South Branch Metedeconk River		Fraction completed
Access Points	**Landmarks**	**Lake Shenandoah to Forge Pond**
Lake Shenandoah		0
N. Hampshire Ave.		1/10
	Power Line	1/2
Rte. 549	GS Pkway	2/3
	No. Branch	
Forge Pond		1
River Rating		B
Canoeing Time, hrs.		3–3.5

There is a quarry off to the right. The South Branch joins the North Branch here. Debris becomes less troublesome and eventually disappears. The river widens to 2 canoe lengths with fewer and more gentle turns. A field of marsh grasses appears on the left and then on the right. An island can be passed on either side; the channel to the right is shorter. Just past the island the left bank of the river forms a spit, which narrows the stream temporarily. Past the spit the river widens to 3 canoe lengths and begins to meander slowly through grasses and a few trees and shrubs. After several turns the channel straightens out and blends into Forge Pond. Reeds covering much of the pond's surface form a pretty corridor almost to the opposite side, where a park offers a good take-out.

River details for the South Branch from Lake Shenandoah to Forge Pond. One may put in either at the dam at Lake Shenandoah or the canoe launch in the park. Cars may not be left at the dam, however, but must be parked in the parking area after gear is unloaded.

Beyond the pool, below the dam, the river narrows quickly to about 1 canoe length. The water is clear, light amber in color, and the current pushes the canoe along quickly over the sandy bottom. The banks consist of dark, sandy soil about 2 to 3 feet above the river. They are heavily covered with hardwoods and underbrush. Debris begins appearing after a few hundred feet, and one may be confronted with an occasional liftover. Maneuvering among the fallen trees is tight; it would make good practice for a slalom.

In about twenty minutes the river crosses under New Hampshire Avenue, beyond which the river becomes braided into narrow channels. At places the vegetation closes in on both sides to such an extent that maneuvering the paddle is impossible, and one must grab the vines and pull oneself and the boat through the water. The current must be observed carefully in order to avoid taking a false channel. Occasionally the vegetation forms a wall and is best negotiated with help of pruning clippers. Grapevines are prominent and fertile; they may make a delicious trip in September if the birds leave some of the fruit.

In about an hour the river flows into the cleared area under a high-voltage power line and picks up additional water from small streamlets. Then the woods close in again, and stumps, logs, grape vines and blackberry bushes are encountered. About forty minutes past the power line is a very large tree, probably requiring a liftover. This is the tree visible from the bridge at Route 549. Just beyond Route 549 is the Garden State Parkway.

After the Parkway, the river is marshy and soon enters a small pond. A quarry is on the right. The North Branch enters from the left and adds to the water flow for the beautiful and relaxing paddle down to the park at the eastern end of Forge Pond. In the summer the pond becomes somewhat choked with weeds, and one may have to look carefully for the route.

~~~~~~

20

Manasquan River

Although a portion of the Manasquan lies within the boundary of the Pine Barrens, it would certainly not be included within the Pines on the basis of its appearance. The only characteristic it shares with the other rivers is its capability for accumulating debris, and even in that respect it differs. The Manasquan is a wide, gently meandering river with medium to high banks that are either gentle and sloppy with mud or steep, rocky and dripping with iron-saturated water. The woods on either side are typical of northern New Jersey. The river's current apparently flows very rapidly in times of high water and then weakens quickly, for its load can be seen deposited in isolated places. In low water one often encounters a collection of debris 4 to 5 feet high that is dense enough, fortunately, to support a canoe dragged across it. I was able to paddle this river only once and, as the reader may have guessed, did not do it in high water, when the river should present few problems. I decided that the best time to canoe the Manasquan would be on a warm day after a season of rain or after a very heavy rainfall.

Nevertheless, the river does have attractive features, the most outstanding of which is the precipitous banks of limonite that are stained with rusty hues and support mountain laurel and beech trees. Another is the section within Allaire State Park, where fine stands of sycamore and holly grow.

Six different Indian origins have been suggested for the word Manasquan. All things considered, the two most likely seem to be *manatahasquawhan,* which meant "stream of the island for squaws," and a combination of *menackhen* and *esquand,* which meant "island" and "door." At the mouth of the river on Osborne Island, known locally as Treasure Island, Indian women and children used to be isolated for safekeeping while the men hunted shellfish.

The Monmouth County Parks Department sponsors canoe races on the Manasquan each year in mid-May. Also, the river is stocked with trout by the state and should be avoided on opening day of the trout fishing season.

Possible routes. The river is navigable from Havens Bridge Road to the Manasquan Wildlife Management Area (WMA). (Above Havens Bridge Road it is clogged, and below the Manasquan WMA it becomes tidal.) The whole run can be made in a long day, but it is best, especially in a time of low water, to break it up into two trips. Several roads cross the river, so the exact route may be juggled according to one's interests. A short, enjoyable trip through Allaire State Park can be made by putting in at Route 547 and paddling from there to the Manasquan WMA. Access at Route 547 is somewhat limited, but it is possible to put in from a service road between the ramps of the Interstate 195 interchange. The best access areas are at Southard Avenue and Preventorium Road, where parking areas are provided for fishing. An excellent access for take-out, better than at the Manasquan WMA, is at the bridge on Hospital Road. This shortens the trip by about a half hour.

Campgrounds.
Allaire State Park
Pine Cone Campground
Turkey Swamp Park

Canoe rental agencies.
Algonquin Adventures

Turkey Swamp Park has rental canoes, but they may be used only at the lake in the park.

Public transportation. None.

Other amenities. Route 9 has many facilities. There are hospitals in Freehold and Neptune.

Water level. At Havens Bridge Road, a retaining wall on one side of the bridge supports a large, concrete drainpipe and makes a convenient measuring reference. On my trip in the fall, the water was 40 inches below the top of the wall. The water level was low; it should reach nearly to the wall's top to be satisfactory. Additionally, there is a gauge station at Route 547. The readings there in the fall were 3.0 feet and 2.0 feet on the upstream and downstream sides of the spillway, respectively.

In early summer the Braleys found the water to be at a summer high. At that time the reading on the upstream gauge at Route 547 was 3.5 feet.

Below Preventorium Road the river has fewer liftovers than upstream; therefore, it is navigable in low water. It is said to be canoeable throughout the year.

River details from Havens Bridge Road to Brice Park. When putting in anywhere along the Manasquan River, one should be careful because the banks are muddy and slippery.

At Havens Bridge Road, the river is 1½ to 2 canoe lengths wide with gentle turns. The banks are medium to high and are covered with leaves and mountain laurel. The other bushes and trees are mostly deciduous, with a few pines. Occasionally, the banks are stained by iron oxide that oozes out of the mud. Patches of debris shift along the river from one flood to another, but in low water there are a dozen of them above Preventorium Road and somewhat fewer downstream. A typical patch of debris is a collection of assorted branches and brush that has accumulated behind a log and extends several feet above the water. In many cases one can push around the debris after freeing some branches to loosen the collection. Otherwise the canoe must be hauled over the top.

A few houses can be seen now and then along the shore. Bushes gradually become more dense and often hang over and dip into the water. Even in a time of low water, the current is moderate to fast. After a short while the river passes under Ketcham Road.

Laurel disappears for a time, and other bushes and grasses are thick along the shore. The banks are occasionally steep, rocky and wet with rust-colored streaks deposited by iron-laden water. Beech trees grow up from the almost vertical banks; some of them stand on exposed roots, the soil having eroded away. Then a row of beehives can be seen on the right shore, and one comes to West Farms Road. The river continues to meander gently between muddy or steep, rocky banks. There are regularly spaced accumulations of debris. Eventually one crosses under Southard Avenue and, a few minutes later, Preventorium Road.

The river begins a short series of sharp and frequent turns. In fifteen minutes or so, it passes under a railroad trestle. Mountain laurel is again evident and contrasts with the gray bark of large, old beech trees that crowd the shore. A type of evergreen honeysuckle sprawls over the bushes and hangs from the trees. Although the current varies from weak to strong, it is usually moderate or stronger, and there are several periods of what is very fast water for the Pine Barrens. After some time the river passes under Route 547. A few feet down-

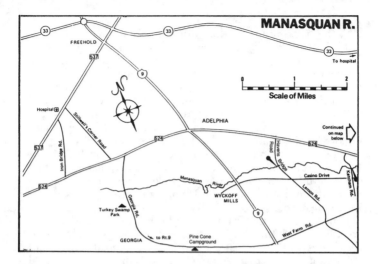

MANASQUAN R.

FREEHOLD

33

537

9

Hospital

Stillwell's Corner Road

Iron Bridge Rd.

537

524

To hospital

Scale of Miles
0   1   2

ADELPHIA

524

Havens Bridge Road

524

Continued on map below

Casino Drive

Lemon Rd.

Ketcham Rd.

Manasquan River

WYCKOFF MILLS

9

Turkey Swamp Park

Georgia Rd.

GEORGIA

to Rt. 9

Pine Cone Campground

West Farm Rd.

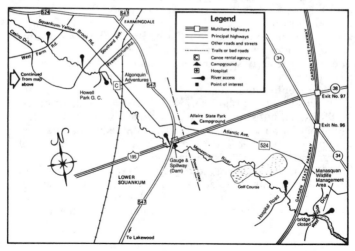

524

547

FARMINGDALE

Squankum-Yellow Brook Rd.

Casino Drive

West Farm Rd.

Southard Ave.

Preventorium Rd.

Legend

≣ Multilane highways
═ Principal highways
── Other roads and streets
- - - Trails or bad roads
C Canoe rental agency
▲ Campground
✚ Hospital
✦ River access
■ Point of interest

34

Continued from map above

Howell Park G. C.

Algonquin Adventures

C

547

Allaire State Park Campground

195

Atlantic Ave.

524

38
Exit No. 97

Exit No. 96

34

LOWER SQUANKUM

547

Gauge & Spillway (Dam)

Manasquan River

Power Lines

Golf Course

Hospital Road

GARDEN STATE PARKWAY

Manasquan Wildlife Management Area

bridge closed

To Lakewood

Manasquan River		Fraction Completed			
Access Points	Land-marks	Havens Bridge Rd. to Manasquan WMA	Havens Bridge Rd. to Preventorium Road	Preventorium Road to Manasquan WMA	Route 547 to Manasquan WMA
Havens Bridge Road		0	0		
Ketcham Road			1/3		
West Farms Road		1/4	2/3		
Southard Avenue		1/3			
Preventorium Road			1	0	
	Railroad trestle	1/2			
Route 547					0
	Power line	2/3		1/2	
	Golf course	5/6		3/4	1/2
Hospital Road		9/10		7/8	3/4
	Brice Park				
Manasquan WMA		1		1	
River Rating		B	A+	A+	A
Canoeing Time, hrs.		4–6½	1½–3	2½–3½	1½–2½

stream there is a gauge station with a concave spillway. At the autumn water level, I was able to run the middle of the spillway with only a modest amount of scraping.

Scant minutes later a high-voltage power line crosses the stream, and very soon the river enters Allaire State Park, as indicated by a sign. Sycamore trees and poison ivy grow well here. The river begins to meander more frequently with turns becoming sharp. The trees, growing close to the river on occasionally swampy banks, arch high overhead and shade one's passage. Eventually, the Manasquan passes under a small, wooden footbridge and through a golf course that is the river's only suitable place for a stop, other than at road crossings.

One crosses under two smaller footbridges and passes a pretty patch of holly. In a half-hour, Hospital Road appears, beyond which is a wooden road bridge. Trees become thinner and bushes are thicker. Soon the river passes under the Garden State Parkway and, a few minutes later, passes through the former Brice Park. It was possible to take out here at one time, but no longer. Just beyond, the river crosses under a barricaded bridge at West Side Drive. Downstream, about 200 yards past the former take-out at the park, is the Manasquan WMA take-out, on the left near a blacktop walkway into the WMA.

NORTHWEST

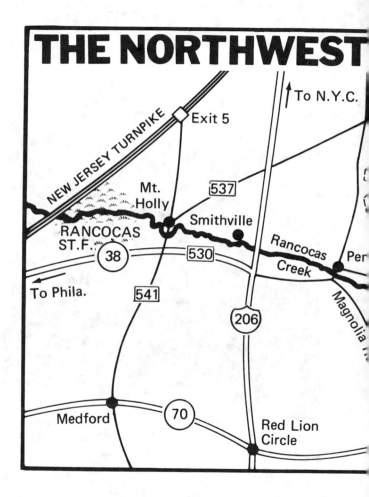

THE NORTHWEST

↑ To N.Y.C.

NEW JERSEY TURNPIKE

Exit 5

537

Mt. Holly

Smithville

RANCOCAS ST.F.

38

530

Rancocas Creek

Per

← To Phila.

541

Magnolia

206

Medford

70

Red Lion Circle

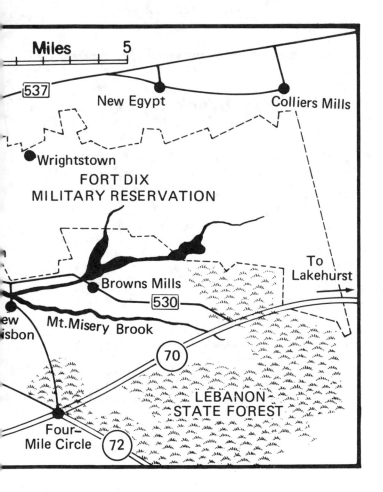

21

Mount Misery Brook

Mount Misery Brook is a narrow, twisting, delightful stream that is bounded by a thin border of mixed trees and bushes behind which fields of pines and scrubby sands are located. Flowing through a panorama of low bushes and marsh grasses and then an abandoned cranberry bog, it converges with Pole Bridge Brook to form the Greenwood Branch of Rancocas Creek. Mount Misery Brook is consistently the narrowest of the navigable rivers in the Pine Barrens. It is not an easy run because of the numerous turns, and the Greenwood Branch sometimes has an extensive amount of debris. But the trip is pretty and is a challenging diversion for those jaded by the standard runs.

Many people believe that Mount Misery is a shortened version of a former name, Mount Misericorde. One author disputes that belief on the ground that Misericorde appears nowhere in the historical records. He claims that the millworkers in the town of Mount Misery used to suffer many hardships during the area's cold winters and named the town accordingly, and that the river is named after the town. Another author believes that the town got its name from the brook and that the brook was named by Indians.

An ironworks was operated for many years on Mount Misery

Brook; the dam that supplied it with power was later converted to form a cranberry bog.

Possible routes. The normal run is from Route 70 to New Lisbon. There is a short canoeable stretch upstream from Route 70, but since its access is on private property and one must have permission to use it, the small amount of extra paddling is not worth the trouble. At New Lisbon there is a crude rock dam that must be lined over or portaged around. That too is not worth the effort unless one wishes to continue downstream on an overnight trip on the Rancocas.

Canoeing from Route 70 to New Lisbon is a good two-day trip, with a stop at Mary Ann Furnace. The lower section is longer and more strenuous. At one time several large, fallen sweet gum trees blocked the passage below Mary Ann Furnace and required liftovers. They were cut away but have since been replaced by a more extensive gauntlet of debris. Someone may be attempting to maintain the river, but paddlers should be prepared to encounter liftovers; a saw and long-handled clippers should be brought along. The lower section is best done on the first day, and the upper section, which is shorter and more attractive, saved for the second day. Mary Ann Furnace is on Mount Misery Road, a poor sandy road coming in from Junction Avenue. This road is barricaded south of the river and is no longer driveable from Route 70. Those drivers who are shuttling cars must take Spring Lake Boulevard to Country Lake Estates, and turn left at Choctaw Drive to get to Route 530. Mount Misery Road has become an informal garbage dump, so it may be difficult to distinguish the tiny bridge at Mary Ann Furnace from the refuse on the road. Fortunately, the river is still reasonably free of litter, except for some garbage around Mary Ann Furnace. Parking at Mary Ann Furnace is limited.

Greenwood Bridge is an alternate take-out to New Lisbon.

The river is free of debris below the bridge, and some people may find it dull after the rigorous passage from Mary Ann Furnace. It would shorten the trip by one to one and a half hours.

Campground.
Lebanon State Forest

Canoe rental agencies. None.

Public Transportation. None.

Other amenities. The small towns of Pemberton and Browns Mills have markets and gas stations. More gas stations are located on Route 72 near Route 70. There are hospitals at Mount Holly, Toms River and Lakewood.

Water level. On my runs, the water at Route 70 was 103 inches below the bridge in the spring and 106 inches in the fall. These measurements were not particularly meaningful, however, because the fall level farther downstream was a whole foot lower than in the spring. The water was satisfactory on both days, although it would not be if it were much lower.

On their trip in the fall, the Braleys also found the water to be 106 inches below the bridge at Route 70. It was 42 inches below the bridge at Mary Ann Furnace. They agree that the river should not be paddled at a lower level.

River details from Route 70 to New Lisbon. The river leaves Route 70 with a fast current and gentle turns, ½ to 1 canoe length wide. Bushes crowd the shore, and a thin band of trees, both cedar and deciduous, lines the low, damp banks. Some of the trees hang close to the water or grow directly out of it. Behind them the ground rises to support the usual low, scrubby bushes and scattered pines. Most debris can be by-passed, except perhaps in early spring, and the chances of a liftover in this section are usually minimal. Subsequently, the already tight passage is further restricted to 1 canoe width. Soon the stream begins to turn very sharply and frequently. A short time later, at the spot where some trees grow out of the water, there is a break in the bushes on the left; it offers a narrow access to an open sandy area that makes an excellent lunch stop for anyone starting late. An interesting lichen can be seen on the sand.

In ten minutes, as the river leaves the woods, the bushes become dense, turns are more gentle and the debris is gone. Scant minutes later, however, the river reenters woods, the turns become sharp once again and debris reappears. Occasionally, a pine field can be seen close to the river, but access to it is hindered by bushes, which also hang over the water and hinder one's passage. A rather strong current adds to the difficulties. The river sometimes diverges around an island; a shortcut is possible if one stays alert. Eventually the trees thin out, and the river passes through an open field of dense mixed bushes, with pines and cedars on the distant shore. It is not swampy—the banks are firm and sandy. The channel is well defined and has a width of 1 canoe length. It meanders, there are many sharp turns and the sandy bottom is clear except for underwater grasses. The bushes alongside present beautiful variations of green, rust and brown, and there are cranberries. Soon the bushes thin out and are replaced by marsh grasses and scattered saplings. A dry, sandy bank appears on the right. Then one is confronted by two felled pine trees blocking the river; they may be difficult to negotiate. Around the next turn, a low-voltage power line crosses the river. A sand ramp on the right leads to a sandy plateau, which is a fine stopping place that provides a panoramic view over the field. This area was probably dammed

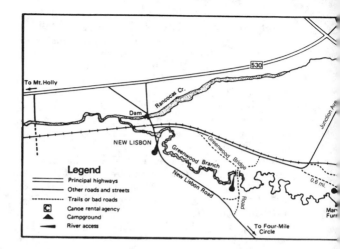

at one time to provide a controlled water supply to the old cranberry field downstream.

A few minutes later one comes upon the ruins of a wooden structure that may have been a dam. Then the river is absolutely straight for several minutes as it evidently follows a canal within the old cranberry farm. The current has weakened and remains so for the rest of the river. Bushes heavily line the banks for a few minutes and then fall back when the banks become swampy. In the cranberry field the river widens to 1½ canoe lengths, and cranberry bushes are everywhere. Shortly, the Pole Bridge Brook flows in from the right. Maple trees begin to grow alongside and shade the river. The water spreads out into ponds partially filled with water lilies and green arrow arum. In a few minutes the river arrives at a second set of wooden ruins—undoubtedly the remains of the

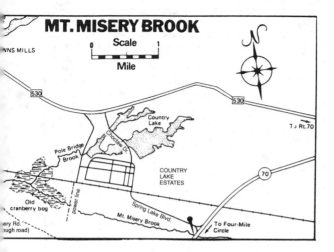

MT. MISERY BROOK

Scale

0 _____ 1

Mile

dam at the foot of the cranberry field. Here there are only pilings and a retaining wall, which are no impediment to a canoe. Within another few minutes, the river passes under the sand road at Mary Ann Furnace. Nearby, many years ago, Mary Ann Furnace produced iron by using power from the water of Mount Misery Brook.

The river widens briefly and then narrows to 1 canoe length. The bushes are very dense and hang over the river; the trees are moderately dense and mostly deciduous. An island temporarily narrows the river to as little as 1 canoe width, and soon there is a very high bank on the right. The amount of debris is moderate, and several liftovers may be necessary. The river begins to meander sharply with frequent turns, except for occasional straight sections of a few minutes. Because the banks are usually swampy, there is no

Mt. Misery Brook		Fraction Completed			
Access Points	Land-marks	Route 70 to New Lisbon	Route 70 to Greenwood Bridge	Route 70 to Mary Ann Furnace	Mary Ann Furnace to New Lisbon
Route 70		0	0	0	
	Trees in water, rest stop, left	1/8	1/7	1/4	
	Powerline	1/3	2/5	8/10	
Mary Ann Furnace		2/5	1/2	1	0
	Beach, R.	3/4	9/10		3/5
Greenwood Bridge Road			1		3/4
New Lisbon		1			1
River Rating		C	C	B	B
Canoeing Time, hrs.		6–9	5–8	2.5–3.5	4–6

200

way to get to the high land in the background where pines can be seen. Patches of ferns alternate with bushes and grasses along the water's edge. At the bend of one turn, three massive sweet gum trees once lay across the river. They have been cut out but are now replaced by a half-dozen large maples, followed by many other trees requiring lift-overs. Paddlers should plan to spend a long time out of the water before getting through this mess.

For the next one to one and a half hours, the river continues in the same fashion: sharp turns, swampy banks supporting bushes, marsh grasses or ferns, many trees and moderate to heavy debris. The river often meanders near a high bank, and occasionally there are places where one can gain access to a flat, dry field of scattered pines, scrub oaks and ferns. A hair-pin turn to the left marks the end of this section; on the outside bank there is an excellent low, sandy beach that appears to be privately owned by a veterans group. It is not posted, how-ever, and rest stops may be permitted if the beach is not disturbed.

Past the beach there is less debris. The turns are still sharp but have long, straight sections in between. In ten or fifteen minutes, a row of pilings appears across the river—the remains of an old bridge. The river widens to 1½ canoe lengths. After a few more minutes, one comes to a cutoff where the water swiftly rushes through a narrow channel in the bushes. Soon the river widens further to 2 canoe lengths. There is little debris here. The turns are gentle and, in another few minutes, the river crosses under the road at Greenwood Bridge. On the downstream side of the bridge is a sandy clearing where local people use the river as a swimming hole.

From here to New Lisbon, the river is wide and the pad-dling is easy, although sharp meanders continue to occur. The banks are high and covered with bushes and trees. Houses begin to appear; they are present till the end. As New Lisbon is approached, the river becomes quite marshy because of a rock dam at New Lisbon Road.

To continue beyond the dam, one must line the canoe over the rocks next to the road. Then there are a few turns. Several houses are located along the shore. In ten minutes the river passes under a bridge and in another five minutes it flows into the North Branch of Rancocas Creek.

22

Rancocas Creek

Anyone who has canoed elsewhere in the Pine Barrens and then tries Rancocas Creek will find it an anomaly. Its differences are profound: except for initial downed wood and several large logs that may necessitate liftovers just below Browns Mills, the Rancocas contains no troubling debris, except perhaps above the lake at the New Lisbon dam. Its trees and bushes are typical of northern New Jersey woods, and its banks are usually firm, not sandy. It is a wide, continually meandering river graced by high banks where towering trees grow. It is easy, pretty and a good stream for beginners. Most of Rancocas Creek lies outside the Pine Barrens; but since a portion is inside, and Mount Misery Brook flows into the creek, I have included the Rancocas for the sake of continuity.

The creek is apparently named after an Indian tribe—which one is not clear. The Remkokes lived along the Delaware River, as did the Ancocus Indians. Mount Holly, on the banks of the Rancocas, is one of the oldest cities in the state, having been settled by Quakers in the late 1600s.

Browns Mills now rivals Whitesville on the Toms River for the filthiest access award. Much of the litter from the parking area washes down the river until it is strained out by the numerous downed trees. This gives us a reason to be grateful for debris in the water.

Possible routes. The river has three tributaries: the North, South and Southwest branches. Only the North Branch has a navigable section within the Pine Barrens; it is the tributary described here. The best run is from Browns Mills to Mount Holly. (Upstream from Browns Mills, the canoeing is mostly over lakes, and below Mount Holly, the river soon becomes tidal.) The entire trip can be made on a very long day, but dividing it into two or more one-day runs is much more compatible with the spirit of the river. Furthermore, the water in the lake behind the dam at New Lisbon was recently lowered to about 4 feet below normal—probably to relieve pressure on the dam, which is in poor condition. This has caused more debris above the dam and made plans for a two-day trip preferable not only spiritually but practically. One possible split is from Browns Mills to Pemberton and from there to Mount Holly. But roads cross the river at several places, so other choices can be made. A saw and clippers may be helpful above the dam at New Lisbon.

There are some open areas where one might try to camp primitively, but I do not know whether it is permitted. Certainly a fire permit would be required for open fires.

Route 206 does not have a suitable access to the river unless canoes are rented there at Jones Canoes. Although Hack's Canoe Retreat has a hauling service, many people paddle upstream and then back down again, which gives the reader a notion of the current that may be expected.

Campground.
Lebanon State Forest

Canoe rental agency.
Hack's Canoe Retreat

Public transportation. From New York City, one can take the Atlantic City Coachways bus to Mount Holly. From Phil-

204

adelphia, one can take the New Jersey Transit bus to Mount Holly. From either bus stop, it is a short walk to Hack's Canoe Retreat.

Other amenities. Mount Holly is the largest city in the area, but Pemberton and Browns Mills are of a respectable size and have markets and gas stations. Route 206 has diners, gas stations and motels. There are hospitals in Mount Holly, Toms River and Lakewood.

Water level. There is a water-level gauge mounted on the downstream side of the bridge in Pemberton. Originally, I scouted the river in two sections in the fall, and the readings were 1.7 feet and 1.65 feet. The best access to the river was downstream of the bridge on the same side as the gauge. Now, however, the best access is upstream, and the gauge may not be easy to find. Another gauge is on the bridge at Browns Mills. The Braleys found that gauge read about 6.0 feet when the gauge at Pemberton read 1.89 feet. Most likely this concern about water is academic on the Rancocas. It is likely to be shallow at only one place—New Lisbon—and the river should be navigable throughout the year.

River details from Browns Mills to Mount Holly. After a large pool of water below the dam at Browns Mills, the river narrows to 1 canoe length. Immediately, a sequence of three heavy logs lies across the river; the canoe may have to be lifted over them. The banks are low, muddy and covered with a dense blanket of bushes and trees that in this section opens only at numerous houses. For the first half-hour or so, there is a moderate amount of debris, and several liftovers are possible. The turns are usually gentle, although some are hairpin. The banks gradually become higher and firmer; the bushes become less dense as short grasses and mosses grow among the trees. The debris

205

soon diminishes as the river widens from 1 to 1 ½ canoe lengths, although liftovers are still likely. There are no more houses now. The channel begins to make large meanders, with long, straight stretches interrupted by sharp turns. The woods are mostly deciduous. After a short while, the bushes become dense again, and along with small trees they hang over the river.

The beginnings of a housing development appear on the right, and then the river immediately widens to 2 canoe lengths. The trees draw back, and the banks become lower; the water often overflows and forms ponds alongside. Several houses appear in one small area. Gradually growing more swampy, the river begins to lose its form. Marsh grasses, water lilies and, in the fall, purple asters stand out. The turns become frequent, and one must take care not to lose the channel by paddling the wrong way into a pond.

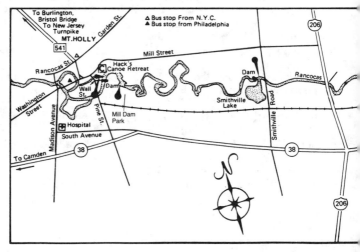

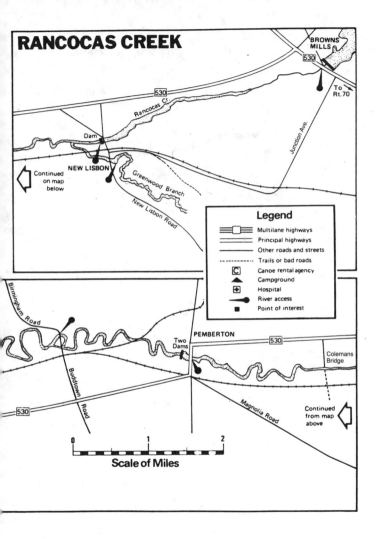

RANCOCAS CREEK

BROWNS MILLS

530

To Rt. 70

530

Rancocas Cr.

Junction Ave.

Dam

NEW LISBON

Greenwood Branch

New Lisbon Road

Continued on map below

Legend

▭	Multilane highways
═══	Principal highways
───	Other roads and streets
------	Trails or bad roads
C	Canoe rental agency
▲	Campground
⊞	Hospital
●	River access
■	Point of interest

Birmingham Road

Buddtown Road

530

Two Dams

PEMBERTON

530

Colemans Bridge

Magnolia Road

Continued from map above

0   1   2

Scale of Miles

Rancocas Creek		Fraction Completed	
Access Points	Landmarks	Browns Mills to Pemberton	Pemberton to Mount Holly
Browns Mills		0	
	River opens up	1/3	
New Lisbon Road		1/2	
	Coleman's Bridge	3/4	
Pemberton		1	0
Brimingham Road			1/4
	Route 206		1/2
	Channel on left		3/4
Mount Holly			1
River Rating		B	A
Canoeing Time, hrs.		3–4	3–4

The river soon opens into the lake at New Lisbon, which is actually like a very wide river because it is exceedingly narrow and long. At the current low water level, docks are high and dry, and stumps show in the water. The best route is in the old river channel. The banks are covered with many varieties of trees (compared with lakeshores farther south where there are mostly pines and cedars), and their fall colors make this lake a pleasure to cross. Several islands lie at the upper end. Soon after entering the lake, one sees a small clearing on the left shore. A strip of trees grows down the middle of the lake for a short distance, dividing it lengthwise. At the trees' end is a wooden dock. Halfway down the lake, the channel narrows to a strait; there is a good stopping place on each side. Then the lake widens and continues to be open until the dam at the New Lisbon Road. At the current low level of the lake, the dam can be portaged by paddling under the bridge, across the face of the dam, to a sandy landing about 5 feet below the top of the retaining wall. Otherwise the canoe must be carried across the highway and put in on the left bank of the river. (The property on both sides of the road is privately owned, but so far the owners appear to permit portaging.)

The river is now 1½ canoe lengths wide, with very little debris. The trees and bushes are dense; some trees arch over the river. On the right bank there is a large farm, and on the left bank are some houses. In a few minutes the Greenwood Branch of the Rancocas flows in from the left, and Rancocas Creek widens to 2 canoe lengths. Past a concrete abutment, there are houses for quite awhile. The river widens to 3 canoe lengths and moves gently along through a corridor of tall overhanging trees and bushes. In a short time a broad, spacious field appears on the left, but it is littered and unattractive. Just downstream, the river passes under Coleman's Bridge, a galvanized bridge that replaced the old wooden bridge whose

209

pilings are still evident in the water. Access to and from the river is barred. The open field on the left continues for ten minutes in a somewhat cleaner condition, with access from the river at two places.

The banks are firm, and several massive oak trees appear. In a few minutes there is a good stopping place on the left. An occasional house can be seen. The river widens further. Gradually, the trees become more slender and less overhanging, and the banks become somewhat marshy. At Pemberton, a power line crosses overhead. A few minutes later, the river enlarges to a small pond and passes under Route 530. The best access is on the left, at a community park upstream from the bridge. It has a parking area and a broad grass lawn.

Beyond the bridge the river forks to pass around an island; a dam across each fork requires a portage. The river is now slightly narrower and continues to meander gently. The banks are firm and often extend 12 feet above the water. Large, handsome trees—beeches, oaks, ironwoods, catalpas—give the impression of northern New Jersey. A tributary enters on the right and, a few minutes later, the Rancocas passes under a railroad trestle.

For a brief period, the right bank is high and steep with numerous large beech trees, whose roots are exposed by soil erosion. For the next fifteen minutes, the banks are covered with a wild growth of slender trees and dense bushes and a tangle of vines and brambles. A lucky paddler may spot a patch of wild grape vines on the left bank, with fruit a cut above the pinched, sour grapes one usually finds in fields upstate. After another section of stately trees, a broad, sloping bank covered with leaves and large trees appears on the right. One could stop anywhere and enjoy a quiet rest. Soon a railroad track passes close by on the left and, a few minutes later, there is a road bridge. A channel leaves the left side of the river here and rejoins it farther downstream; but the channel may be too shallow for canoeing—it was when I tried it. Soon, the Rancocas passes under a second bridge, at Birmingham Road.

The riverbanks here are low but still firm, with short grasses and moss growing among young, slender trees. In a few minutes one passes the spot on the left where the channel returns to the river. Just past it is a chemical factory, which may give off an unpleasant smell. Past that, a wooden bridge crosses the river. Several minutes later another pretty stand of beech trees extends along the right bank for some distance, following which the river meanders around a peninsula and passes a long string (about ten minutes' worth) of densely packed houses. Then there are scattered houses and trees on both banks for 15 minutes, until the river crosses under Route 206.

West of Route 206, the river becomes very wide and open, with low banks. In a few minutes it passes under a high-voltage power line. A farm appears on the right. On the left is a good stopping place that is accessible at three spots and, just downstream, the river goes under Smithville Road. Soon the river diverges: The current flows straight ahead to a dam and a power station, and a channel goes left to Smithville Lake, which is a backup reservoir for the station. The dam must be portaged.

A local historical note: During the late 1800s, the world's only bicycle railway ran between Smithville and Mount Holly. Mounted on a fence, its grooved metal track was equipped with fence-straddling high-wheel bicycles that accommodated one to four passengers. Hezekiah B. Smith, the founder of Smithville and owner of a machine plant there, constructed the railway so workers could commute from Mount Holly to the plant by bicycle. The railway operated for several years but was abandoned after Smith's death.

The river now has a width of 2 canoe lengths and follows a slowly meandering course. Trees arch gracefully over the water. After a short time a very long island appears; the main

211

channel flows to the right. A number of houses can be seen along the shore. Gradually, the banks become lower and very bushy, and scrub growth is more common than trees, which are themselves more scraggly than before. In some places marsh grasses grow in the water. Soon there is a narrow spit of bushes on the left separating the main channel from a large bay in which water birds may sometimes be seen.

In a few minutes the river widens to more than 3 canoe lengths and diverges around several small islands. The banks are very swampy. Houses appear frequently, signifying the outskirts of the city of Mount Holly. In the distance, beyond the city, the top of the mountain itself is visible. It is an almost surrealistic sight to a person accustomed to the lowlands of the Pine Barrens. Shortly, the river passes under a footbridge. The river then turns left and goes over a dam. Private paddlers may take out above the dam on the left, at a public launch in Mill Dam Park. Those renting canoes from Hack's Canoe Retreat should paddle along the millrace (a narrow canal to the right of the dam) for a short distance to Hack's, on the right. Private paddlers may also run the race and take out on the left, but it's a long way to the parking area.

SOUTH

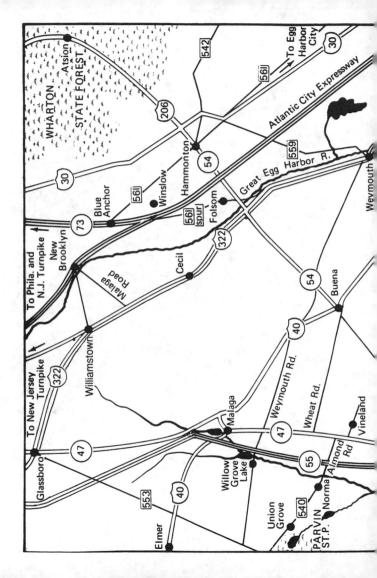

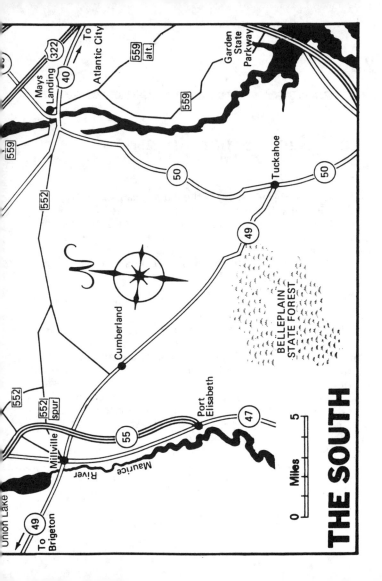

THE SOUTH

0 Miles 5

23

~~~~~~

Great Egg Harbor River

The Great Egg Harbor River is the longest canoeable river in the Pine Barrens. The upper section is wild and strewn with logs. It is a strenuous run, but it has a powerful attraction for canoeists, who persist in efforts to keep it open. In the nineteenth century the river was kept clear for commercial reasons. In *Exploring the Little Rivers of New Jersey,* the Cawleys note a traveler's 1907 recollection of a boat ride down the Great Egg at a time when the river was free of the rubble that is common today. A decade or so ago, a local resident frequently took his wife for a day trip on the upper section. He kept the river clean single handedly by rowing a boat upstream and sawing debris as he came to it. Now the river is maintained by members of the South Jersey Canoe Club, although now and then they find 3- and 4-inch trees cleared by an unknown individual.

The beauty of the upper section makes up for the labor. The river passes through a great, continuous swamp that is shaded more heavily than any other Pine Barrens stream. Live trees and dead logs are entangled in contorted, moss-covered masses. Some trees are supported by only half their root systems; others, fallen down, lie with roots high in the air. Great sheets of brier that drape over dense bushes and hang like Spanish moss provide an additional wilderness touch. One can

216

drift happily through this jungle and watch the bubbles on the water and the sun shining through the trees and backlighting the leaves. For those people who like isolation and canoeing as a pleasure in itself, paddling down the upper Egg Harbor River is an enjoyable experience.

Much of the upper section, down to Piney Hollow Road, is now owned by the state and has become the Winslow Wildlife Management Area.

Between Penny Pot and Weymouth, the river cuts through a ridge. As a result, banks are high, trees are firmly rooted and debris is minimal. In contrast to the swamp upstream, this is one of the easiest and most relaxing sections of river in the Pine Barrens.

Below Weymouth the river resumes its swampy nature, except that it is much wider. The approach to Lake Lenape is very pretty, with a panorama of marshes, holly and cedars. This portion of the river is in the new and developing Atlantic County Park at Lake Lenape. The park has campsites, a boat launch, parking and a picnic area, and there are plans to establish swimming areas, nature trails and a visitors center.

The river takes its name from its harbor. When the Dutch settled south Jersey, they named a portion of it *Eyren Haven,* "Egg Harbor," after the great quantity of gull and mud-hen eggs they found in salt meadows during breeding season. The British adopted the translation but named the body of water at the mouth of this river *Great* Egg Harbor, and that between Tuckerton and Long Beach Island *Little* Egg Harbor, because of the relative size of the local eggs. Despite its deceptive name, Great Egg Harbor is the smaller harbor of the two. The name Penny Pot seems to have come from the Dutch word *Paanpacht,* meaning "low, soft land" or "leased land."

An ironworks, powered by the Great Egg, once operated at Weymouth. Weymouth was also a center of charcoal production. Mays Landing, downstream, was an important port and

217

shipbuilding center and, during the Revolution, the scene of a British landing in retaliation for privateering by rebels along the Atlantic Coast.

Possible routes. An easy day's run lies between Penny Pot and Weymouth. The best access is actually not at Penny Pot but at the county park at Eighth Street, just before Penny Pot. For clarity, however, the Eighth Street access will be considered the same as Penny Pot. The riverbanks in Penny Pot are privately owned. Route 322, known locally as "Black Horse Pike," is a busy road and does not offer a safe access; besides, parking on the shoulder is prohibited.

Below Weymouth the river is swampy with debris, but it is canoed often and is kept reasonably clear. One may paddle all the way to Mays Landing or shorten the run and avoid Lake Lenape by taking out at the Winding River Campgrounds. The county may someday set up an access downstream from Winding River Campgrounds. Anyone who does intend to be on the lake, whether with boats or canoes, should register with the Park at Mays Landing and leave the name and phone number of a contact person. This is a good safety policy; strong winds come up unexpectedly on the lake, and in the past the park has had to rescue canoeists.

On the upper section, a good day's run is from New Brooklyn Lake to Piney Hollow Road or, for a shorter journey, from Winslow—Williamstown Road to Piney Hollow Road. The run from Piney Hollow Road to Penny Pot is standard.

There is less debris on the river now than about ten years ago, but still, a saw and pruning clippers are advisable above Piney Hollow Road. A recent blowdown could make them useful.

Campgrounds.
Indian Branch Park Campground
Winding River Campgrounds

Indian Branch Park Campground is located about ¼ mile from the river and can be reached from a beach controlled by the campground. Camping is not permitted on the beach itself. Winding River Campgrounds is situated on the river.

There are several dry, sandy banks along the Great Egg that are unposted. Camping might possibly be allowed in these spots as long as they are left unlittered and undisturbed.

Camping is prohibited, however, within the Winslow Wildlife Management Area and also in any county park where camping is not specifically provided for. This eliminates the portions upstream of Piney Hollow Road (the Blue Hole area is patrolled regularly) and downstream of Weymouth except at established campgrounds.

Canoe rental agencies.
Bel Haven Lake (hauling only if trucks are not already busy in the Wharton Tract)
Lampe's Canoe Rental
Lenape Park Recreation Center
Winding River Campgrounds

Public transportation. None.

Other Amenities. Hammonton is a city; Mays Landing is a medium-sized town. Route 322 has numerous motels, dining places, gas stations and an occasional market. There is a hospital in Hammonton.

Water level. There is a gauge station at Route 54, on the upstream end of the left retaining wall, behind the gauge station building. A portion of the gauge had disappeared at the time I scouted the river, and I relied on the water passing over the spillway at the gauge station as a guide to river conditions above Penny Pot; from the thin sheet of water I inferred dif-

219

ficult conditions. The Braleys think otherwise, however, and I defer to their judgment: For suitable conditions above Route 54, the water should be 50 inches or less under the new bridge at New Brooklyn; 3.6 feet or more at the (new) gauge at the Winslow-Williamstown Road; or 2 inches or more higher than the base of the cross braces on the bridge at Piney Hollow Road. At lower water the number of liftovers above the Winslow-Willamstown Road is likely to double at least, and the situation may be comparable between there and Route 54.

A gauge is also on the downstream side of the bridge at Route 322, below Weymouth. It is not worth the trouble to check, although the Braleys did note a reading of 2.95 feet as they paddled by it. In practice, the water level is nearly always sufficient below Penny Pot because of the additional water flowing from Hospitality Creek. In exceptionally dry periods, the water may be shallow below Weymouth.

River details from New Brooklyn Lake to Mays Landing. Below the lake the river is narrow and impeded by fallen trees. It soon broadens to 1½ canoe lengths. The banks are continually water-soaked, and more fallen trees lie about in all directions. Masses of upturned roots with soil clinging to them project a dozen feet into the air, and mushrooms may occasionally be found in the soil among the roots. A power line from across New Brooklyn Lake parallels the river until well past the point where the river passes under the Atlantic City Expressway, about twenty minutes from the lake. Then a second power line can be seen ahead, and the considerable debris in its vicinity may require a liftover. After weaving through bushes in the water, one crosses the power line right-of-way— a graded sand road that has been eroded through by the river. Here and farther on, the river swells out into the swamp at times of high water and makes the channel difficult to follow.

The river meanders gently through the swamp. There are

heavy patches of debris, many of which will require a liftover, depending upon water level and the latest clearing efforts. Deciduous trees, mostly maples with a very occasional holly, arch over and shade the river. Mosses and lichens grow on the trees. Dense bushes hang over the water and narrow the channel. Brier grows here and there and dangles into the water from the bushes. I have seen no poison ivy on this upper section of the Great Egg, except for a patch or two below Route 54. Its absence may be explained by the small amount of sunlight that penetrates the canopy of trees. About one and a half to two hours after the Atlantic City Expressway, the river crosses under Winslow-Williamstown Road.

The debris becomes infrequent for some time, perhaps twenty minutes; it may be worse, however, in early spring. In times of high water, the river tends to spread out through the trees, but at lower levels one can find an occasional flat, grassy spot that may be dry enough for a stop. Soon debris is more frequent and may necessitate an occasional liftover. Long, straight passages are broken by tight turns. Although an island sometimes narrows the channel, the width of the river remains constant at 1½ canoe lengths. An occasional growth of holly begins to appear. Gradually, debris occurs in heavier patches; pushing through the brush may take ten minutes at one place and half an hour at another. After a distinct lessening of debris, a stand of cedar appears on the left, followed by the sloping sand bank at Blue Hole.

At one time a bridge crossed the river at Blue Hole. On the left there is an extensive, cleared sandy area, surrounded by pines. Fishermen drive here from Piney Hollow Road. On the right bank, a narrow path leads to a broad, deep excavation filled with water. When the river overflows after a heavy rain, it carries fresh water to the hole, thus keeping it reasonably free from stagnation.

The river is laden with trash for some distance downstream

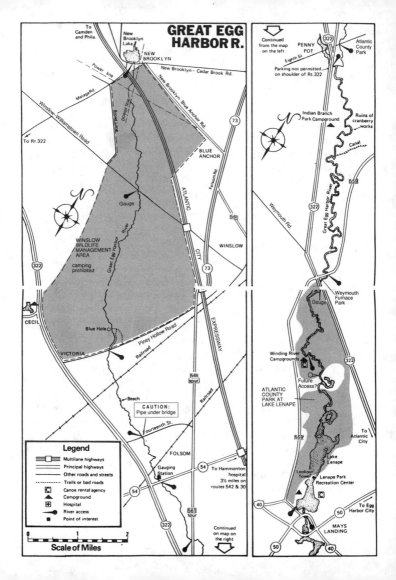

Great Egg Harbor River		Fraction Completed			
Access Points	Landmarks	New Brooklyn Lake to Mays Landing	New Brooklyn Lake to Piney Hollow Road	Winslow-Williamstown Rd. to Piney Hollow Rd.	Winslow-Williamstown Rd. to 14th Street
New Brooklyn		0	0		
Winslow-Williamstown Rd.			1/3	0	0
	Blue Hole	1/3	9/10		
Piney Hollow Road		2/5	1	1	3/5
	Trestle				7/10
	Stop				
14th Street		1/2			1
	Trestle				
Route 54		3/5			
	Route 561 Spur				
8th Street		2/3			
	Penny Pot				
	Cranberry Bog Ruins				
	Route 559				
Weymouth		4/5			
	Winding River Camp	9/10			
	Enter Lake Lenape				
Mays Landing		1			
River Rateing		C	C	B	B–C
Canoeing Time, hrs.		Several Days	5.5–7	4–5	5–6

Great Egg	Fraction Completed			
Access / Landmarks	Piney Hollow Rd. to 8th Street	Route 54 to Weymouth	8th Street to Weymouth	Weymouth to Mays Landing
New Brooklyn				
Winslow-Will Rd.				
Blue Hole				
Piney Hollow Rd.	0			
Trestle				
Stop	1/3			
14th Street	2/3			
Trestle				
Route 54	1	0		
Route 561		1/5		
8th Street		1/3	0	
Penny Pot		1/2	1/8	
Cranberry Bog Ruins			1/3	
Route 559		9/10	4/5	
Weymouth		1	1	0
Winding River Camp				1/2
Lake Lenape				3/4
Mays Land.				1
River Rate	B	B	A	B
Time, hrs.	3–4	4.5–5.5	3–4	3–4

of Blue Hole, which may partially explain why this area is patrolled.

Liftovers may be necessary, depending on the water level. The left bank is high and sloping. In half an hour, Piney Hollow Road crosses the river. Past its bridge are a quarry on the left bank and a sandy beach on the right.

Below the quarry, the banks are open, with only thin trees on both sides, although there are still masses of bushes. In a few minutes, the debris may be considerable, and the turns are sharper. The river spreads out over the banks here in times of high water. Occasionally, one can see pine trees nearby or in the distance. A half-hour later, the river flows under a railroad trestle and past an open area.

The river heads into dense woods and flows through a heavy patch of debris that lasts for twenty minutes. It then meanders through a clear section where there is a fine sandy beach on the left bank that is perfect for a rest stop. Through there the channel may be washed out when the water is high, which makes for less severe debris.

A few minutes later debris is heavy once again, and turns are often very sharp. Soon a cleared area appears on the left bank, followed shortly by the edge of a housing development on the right. The river diverges around an island. The left channel is usually blocked by an underwater wooden wall; the right channel is shallow at first but deepens and follows alongside the houses to a good access point at the Fourteenth Street Road.

The channel turns left through the woods, paralleling the Fourteenth Street Road, and at the end of the island it passes under the Fourteenth Street bridge. When paddling under the bridge, be sure to duck under the large pipe suspended beneath it; the pipe may not be visible in the shadows. More debris appears, and the river twists sharply, with some hairpin turns. In times of high water, the channel may be difficult to

225

follow. After some time one arrives at a second railroad trestle. Gradually, the trees thin out. The widening of the river and the appearance of grasses along the shore signal the approach of a pond behind a spillway and the Route 54 bridge.

Running the spillway is risky because if it is not done properly, the canoe will turn broadside in the backwater below and roll over. Also, there may not be enough water flowing over the spillway. Anyone determined to try it should first move toward the bow, so that the stern is less likely to hang up, and then back up to a good running distance and paddle hard forward over the spillway, keeping the boat lined up with the current. Otherwise, the canoe should be lined over the spillway or portaged over the highway. There is a small but good beach on the other side where people sometimes swim.

Downstream from the spillway, the channel is very straight at first. The trees are dense along the bank. In a few minutes one comes upon an open area on the left, with a table and bench, and a tiny island where one tree grows. The river continues with patches of debris; some are very heavy and require liftovers. An occasional pine tree can be seen. Turns become frequent and sharp. The banks are not as swampy as those upstream. After one patch of debris approaching Route 561 Spur, a poor, narrow canoe access on the right bank leads to a field of pines. A few minutes later the river passes under the bridge of Route 561 Spur.

Although debris continues to require liftovers, there are not as many, and turns are easier and less frequent. Soon one comes to a level field of pines on the right, cleared of bushes, followed by a sloping field on the left, and then a large house with an arched bridge over the river. At a second large house, the river is channeled between two retaining walls. A half-hour later, there is a low beach on the right with access to a broad, open field. Eventually, one passes under the Eighth Street bridge just before coming into Penny Pot. The county access and park are just below the bridge. To take out, stay to the right around the island.

Depending on the water level, one more liftover may be necessary between here and Penny Pot. The turns gradually become very sharp. Pines and cedars grow along the banks, and there is an access on the left to a broad, weedy field. Soon the river abruptly widens as the Hospitality Creek flows into the Great Egg from the right at Penny Pot.

Hospitality Creek is held back by a dam, and one may easily see it by paddling under Route 322 and continuing a short distance up the creek. It is not especially attractive, but it is historic, being constructed of teakwood salvaged from wrecked ships. Below the dam, the creek sluggishly carries suds from the splashing water through beds of pickerel weed and other water plants into the Great Egg.

The run from Penny Pot to Weymouth is altogether different from anything upstream. The river widens to 3 canoe lengths and flows in slow meanders almost completely clear of debris, save for an occasional log or branch. The banks are generally high and sandy, with several very good places to stop. Unfortunately for canoeists desiring solitude, there are many dwellings in the vicinity. But where the banks are undisturbed by construction, the typical upland vegetation grows: scattered pines, scrub oaks, blueberries and huckleberries, ferns, an occasional sheep laurel and creeping heaths. The Great Egg is now an easygoing river, open to the sun and sky. Only gentle paddling is required.

A least a half-dozen sandy banks appear during the next hour. One very low, broad bank is located on the right, thirty-five minutes after Penny Pot. Picnicking is allowed on the beach, but not camping. To camp, one follows first a sand road and then a paved road that leads to the Indian Branch Park Campground.

Downstream, mounted on the left bank, an abandoned rig

appears—a wooden retaining wall, a rusted, gas-powered water pump, and farther along, a large, rusted conduit. Behind
the bank there is an abandoned cranberry bog that once was
irrigated and drained by the rig. A half-hour later, a canal from
another cranberry bog connects with the river on the left.

Soon the banks become low and swampy or covered in thick
bushes that bar access. Patches of cedars appear, and then the
banks become firm again. The river passes briefly alongside
Route 559. Two more stopping places in pine fields may be
found on the right. A few minutes later, the increasing frequency of houses marks the approach into Weymouth. The
Great Egg passes around the houses in a hairpin turn and
arrives at two bridges. The first carries the millrace to an old
paper mill, of which only the chimney remains. Take care in
paddling here: The river's fast current and sharp curve and the
rubble left from the old dam for Weymouth Furnace often
create a brief white-water section as the river sweeps around
the park. The second bridge allows the river to pass under
Route 559 and alongside Weymouth Furnace Park.

Named after a town in England, Weymouth was once noted
for its iron furnace and forge. The park is part of the Atlantic
County Park at Lake Lenape. It is an excellent place to stop for
a rest but may be crowded on weekends. A spring in the park
is a popular source of drinking water among the residents.

The river is broad and shallow for a few minutes, and then
it passes under Route 322. Considerable debris along the banks
reminds one of the primitive nature of the river. The trees are
again deciduous but thinner than in the upper section; brier is
uncommon. In a few minutes there is a grassy bank on the left
that is good for a stop, but a few more minutes bring one to a
broad, sandy beach on the right that is a much better place and
has a trash can.

Now debris begins to increase, and logs lie across the water.
Turns are very frequent. The river becomes more swampy and

spreads out around bushy islands; one should look carefully to find the best route. It is still wide, about 2 canoe lengths, but several patches of brush, grasses and logs occur, requiring a half-dozen liftovers in an hour. Locally, sweet gum trees are common, with their decorative pendants in the spring and attractive leaves in the summer and fall. Eventually, one should see a house on the left and, a few minutes later, a low, sandy bank. Soon a house appears on the right, and then the wooden dock of the Winding River Campgrounds.

The journey from here to Mays Landing requires about two hours of continuous paddling in quiet water, but if the wind is strong, the passage across Lake Lenape before reaching Mays Landing is very strenuous.

Five minutes downstream from the Winding River Campgrounds, around a bend, there is a beautiful beach. At one time it was a Girl Scout camp, but it is now part of the county park at Lake Lenape and is being developed to include a boat launch. It is a good rest stop and should soon be an alternate take-out before the lake. An old footbridge crosses the river, but at present the supports on the left bank are gone. it is likely to be either rebuilt or taken down.

The river now widens further to 3 canoe lengths and has long, straight sections and few turns. Dense bushes line the shore; marsh grasses grow along the water's edge. The trees are thin, with fields of pines here and there. Holly is common, sometimes mixed with pines but usually growing in patches along the banks. Not long after the Scouts' beach, on the left, a narrow inlet leads to a bay lined with leatherleaf bushes and backed by pines. It is worth a small side trip if one has the time. On the far side, a channel connects the bay with a pond bounded by rushes where water lilies grow.

The Great Egg continues in a large, hairpin meander and arrives, on the left, at a stand of grasses separating the channel from another bay. The river then becomes very wide as it passes through pines and cedars. On the left bank two narrow, sandy openings lead to a field of pines. Narrow side channels begin to split off from the main channel and pass around many small, grassy islands. The river bears left and opens up into a beautiful wide pond, which initially is filled with grasses but later is clear. It is best to paddle across the center of the pond to the opposite shore, which is covered with pines and cedars, and then to bear right to the inlet connecting the pond with Lake Lenape.

At this point, there is no choice but to pass through the inlet and head down the lake; the lookout tower on the left shore is a good landmark. The take-out is the ramp for the county park, which is to the right of the dam at the far end, beyond the campsites on the right shore. Staying to the right side of the lake should avoid most of the water traffic from powerboats and jet skis.

24

Maurice River

The Maurice resembles the Toms River and the Great Egg Harbor River because it runs a tortuous path through a predominantly deciduous forest and it may have many blowdowns. But there are differences: It is shorter; there is a charming run upstream, into Willow Grove Lake; several sandy beaches are in the middle section; and the lower end has most of the debris. Additionally, a number of magnolia trees grow on its banks and remain green almost throughout the year.

The river was named after the Dutch ship *Prince Maurice* (itself named in honor of the Dutch general, Prince Maurice of Orange-Nassau), which was sunk at the river's mouth. Earlier, it had been called the Wahatquenack River. The Cawleys claim that the correct pronunciation of the river is "Morris." With all due respect, I must refute them, based on a run-in with local residents who thought, when I said "Morris," that I was referring to some town in northern New Jersey. The locally definitive way to pronounce the name is "Maah'ris." There would be no trouble if we stayed with Wahatquenack.

The Maurice lies along the southern edge of the Pine Barrens and is adjacent to three cities of respectable size. Glassboro was and still is the glass-manufacturing center of New Jersey. Vineland, once merely a grape-growing center, has become cosmopolitan; it is the birthplace of Welch's grape juice and the Mason jar. And Millville, originally built in support of a number of mills along the river, is now a major producer of holly trees and glass.

Possible routes. The Maurice is fed by several tributaries, the largest of which is Scotland Run. Most of the year one can put in on Scotland Run at Malaga and canoe to Route 552 (Sherman Avenue) at the upper end of Union Lake. Until recently, Union Lake could be paddled, but it was drained to rebuild the dam at Millville. In addition, it is now a "Superfund" site, owing to arsenic contamination from a former chemical plant upstream on one of the lake tributaries. As a remedy, the Environmental Protection Agency (EPA) decided upon a sequential series of cleanup measures along the tributary, with the final effort at the lake no earlier than 1997.

Upstream from Malaga and on the other tributaries, the streams are narrow and often shallow. I tried once to put in on Scotland Run at two places shown on the Pitman East USGS quadrangle. Just below Wilson Lake paddling was impossible because the river lost its banks there and flowed through bushes. At Washington Avenue the river was extremely narrow at first but soon widened comfortably and would have offered a good ride had the water been higher. Unfortunately, I had to take out at the next road crossing, Grant Avenue, so I do not know the nature of Scotland Run between that point and Malaga.

According to the Braleys, Grant Avenue is now another of those ubiquitous informal dumps, and the water at the river is so littered that no one would want to paddle there. With sufficient water, however, a fair access is located at a railroad bridge about 100 yards downstream from Route 47. Access at Route 47 itself is not feasible, owing to heavy traffic. The railroad bridge can be reached by taking a dirt road off Route

47, opposite Pennsylvania Avenue, at the north end of the Franklin Township Municipal Building property. Follow the railroad right-of-way to the stream. At Malaga Lake, canoes may be unloaded at the dam on Route 40, but parking is prohibited. The best parking is at a parking area for fishermen, about a half-mile up the lake off Delsea Drive. Canoes may be put in there or at the dam on Route 40. It is simpler to put in at the parking area, but that requires carrying the canoe across Route 40.

The run from Malaga to Sherman Avenue could be a long run for one day, depending on one's paddling experience. But the river has several access points and can be easily divided into shorter trips. For a weekend, one can paddle from Malaga to Route 540 in Vineland on the first day, and from there to Sherman Avenue on the second.

An overnight trip on the river can be hazardous. There is a good beach upstream from Route 540, but it is accessible by road, and several years ago a group of canoeists was harassed by vandals. There are two more beaches below Landis Avenue, but they are close to Route 55, and one would hear cars driving by throughout the night.

At the present time, Scotland Run and the Maurice River are almost completely clear of logs and brush from the outlet at Malaga Lake to Sherman Avenue. This is largely due to the efforts of the South Jersey Canoe Club and Carl Lampe, the owner of Lampe's Canoe Rentals, and his son Russ; collectively, they clear the river several times a year. Above Malaga Lake, debris should be expected.

Campground.
Parvin State Park

Canoe rental agency.
Lampe's Canoe Rentals

Public transportation. From New York, the Atlantic City Coachways bus goes to Vineland. From Philadelphia, one may take the New Jersey Transit bus to Mount Holly, and then walk to High Street and up High to Rancocas Road—about two blocks in all—to catch the Atlantic City Coachways bus from New York. The problem is that the bus trip is long, and the Maurice River has no established riverbank campground. It may be possible to arrange in advance with Lampe's Canoe Rentals for transportation to and from Parvin State Park.

Other amenities. Glassboro, Millville and Vineland are cities that can supply almost any service required. Route 47 has gas stations and markets. There are hospitals in Vineland and Millville.

Water level. There is a gauge station on Route 540, with a gauge on the upstream side of the spillway. The readings were 2.6 feet in the spring and 2.7 feet in the fall. On both of my trips the water level was low, so the river was sometimes shallow and the current was sluggish.

When I tried the upper Scotland Run in the fall, the water level was 74 inches below the bridge at Washington Avenue and 47 inches below the bridge at Grant Avenue. It should probably be at least 6 inches higher to be canoeable.

During the Braleys' run, the water level was medium, and the gauge read 3.00 feet. The water was 69 inches below the railroad bridge downstream from Route 47 and 55 inches below the bridge at West Garden Road.

River details from the railroad bridge near Route 47 at Malaga to Sherman Avenue (Route 522). Scotland Run, at this point, is about 1 canoe length wide and remains so to Malaga Lake. It flows through mainly deciduous woods. Several logs

234

requiring liftovers are likely to be encountered before the river widens and enters the marsh above Malaga Lake. This is a delightful area; the channel meanders among marsh plants which are often in bloom, especially in August. About halfway down the lake is the access area for fishing, which is suitable for a rest stop. The carry across Route 40 is at the white bridge over the dam, toward the left at the bottom (south) end of the lake. Be careful in crossing Route 40.

Scotland run then leaves Malaga under a canopy of deciduous trees and bushes. Two beautiful red mulberry trees grow on the bank at the put-in, and their delicious fruit colors the ground purple in early June. The width of the river is again just 1 canoe length initially but thereafter is 1½ lengths. The river meanders gently and, in a few minutes, passes under Route 55. The trees become thinner, and the view is blocked only by thick shrubbery along the banks. Soon the bushes also thin out and are replaced by marsh grasses and water plants. The river passes by the concrete ruins of a bridge.

Briefly, the bushes are so dense that they hang far over the water. The banks are low and swampy. An occasional cedar tree can be seen. The bushes are gradually mixed with, and then replaced by, marsh grasses. Stands of cedar become common. For a few minutes the grasses are so thick that they narrow the channel to 3 canoe widths. Then the river opens up into a broad marsh that precedes the clear water of Willow Grove Lake. In the marsh the water flows everywhere through grasses, leatherleaf bushes, irises and water lilies. Near the end of this foliage, there is an extensive open field on the left shore that is good for a stop.

The trip across Willow Grove Lake to Weymouth Road is short. At the road there are two small dams, each with a white bridge. Canoes should be taken out at the bridge on the right and carried across the road; the poison ivy on the other side should be avoided. This is the beginning of the Maurice River,

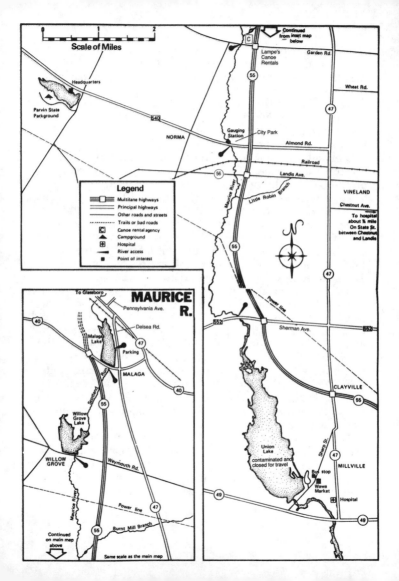

Maurice River		Fraction Completed		
Access Points	Landmarks	Malaga to Route 552	Malaga to Route 540	Route 540 to Route 552
Malaga		0	0	
Weymouth Road			1/4	
	Power line	1/4		
Garden Rd.			2/3	
Beach		1/2		
Route 540			1	0
Landis Avenue				
	Beach	2/3		
	Power line	3/4		2/5
Route 552		1		1
Millville				
River Rating		B+	A	B
Canoeing Time, hrs.		4½–6½	2½–3½	2–3

237

after Scotland Run combines with two smaller tributaries at Willow Grove Lake.

Past the pool of water below the bridge, the river measures 1½ canoe lengths wide, except where it diverges around an island. The banks are low, and water occasionally washes out into the woods. Debris is rare in the fall, but it may hamper passage in the spring until someone cleans it out. The grasses are gone, replaced by bushes and brier overhanging the river-banks. There is some scattered holly. Rather dense trees lean or arch over the water. The river turns frequently and sharply. A number of islands cause the water to divide into several channels; usually only one is navigable. Occasionally, grasses are visible under the water. A fine stand of holly appears, and a few minutes later, the river crosses under a high-voltage power line. The islands cause the channel to become very narrow, and sometimes it shrinks to 1 canoe width. A tributary, the Burnt Mill Branch, flows into the Maurice from the left, and soon after that one crosses under West Garden Road. Lampe's Canoe Rentals is located on Burnt Mill Branch, off West Garden Road; a sign on the river at the confluence directs customers up the side stream.

The river meanders constantly in turns that are very sharp and frequent. Trees crowd over the water. The banks are low, damp and usually crowded with bushes, but sometimes there is a damp grassy area cleared of shrubbery. The channel is 1½ canoe lengths wide. Although debris is only occasional, a lift-over may be necessary. Some time later, the river meanders twice toward a high, pine-topped bank. Just after the second meander, one may see, if it is still there, a hornets' nest suspended high over the water from a tree. The river slowly increases to 2 canoe lengths wide until it diverges around a large island. Several minutes later one passes a broad, sandy beach with a graveled parking lot behind it. A short time later a municipal beach appears on the left, and then the river crosses under Route 540. The gauge station and spillway lie immediately downstream of the bridge. In a time of low water, one should creep under the bridge, staying to one side, and then prepare to line the canoe over the spillway. In a time of high water, it may not be possible to float under the bridge at all.

Now the river is 3 canoe lengths wide and quite straight for several minutes, until a railroad trestle is reached. Then it narrows to 2 canoe lengths and turns occur less frequently. In another few minutes, the river passes under Landis Avenue.

The river makes a constantly curving meander through bushes and trees. In a short time a broad, sandy beach with a steep bank appears on the left within a short walk of Landis Avenue and within earshot of Route 55. Landis Avenue is a possible take-out for emergency purposes, but other places are more convenient. A second beach, narrower and steeper, appears a few yards from the first one. Then a tributary, the Little Robin Branch, flows in from the left. Debris begins to occur more frequently, the result of large trees falling across the river. The banks are low and swampy, but the river occasionally meanders near a field of pine trees, and sometimes one can spot a way into the field for a rest stop. The water often weaves through islands, and at one point the channel is very narrow. After some time the river crosses under a low-voltage power line.

The debris becomes more severe as the Maurice begins to resemble the upper Great Egg Harbor River, with its tangled mass of large trees. However, few if any liftovers should be necessary. Heavy stands of brier increase the similarity; holly and poison ivy are common. The gentle turns go unappreciated because of the large amount of debris. At one point most of the mess stops, and the river suddenly widens to 4 canoe lengths for several minutes, but it is only temporary. There is more debris, and then the river flows under Sherman Avenue.

25

~~~~~~

New Adventures

Many small streams and attractive lakes in the Pine Barrens are little known except as landmarks of the popular rivers. If you want to try something new and, in some cases, are willing to take your chances, you may be well rewarded.

Lake Canoeing

Canoeists who prefer lakes to rivers should find a large number of lakes to their liking in the Pine Barrens. All of them are artificial, but some are three hundred years old. They were created when the rivers were dammed to provide power for sawmills and, later, ironworks, gristmills, paper mills and glassworks. The vegetation has had time to adapt to the lakes and recover from the disturbances of the various industries. Canoeing on a lake for a few hours can be very pleasant. I have occasionally seen people fishing.

The following list of lakes is classified according to region and to each lake's river. Only lakes with good access appear in the list. For more information, see individual river descriptions.

Wharton State Forest

Mullica River

- Goshen Pond: Small but pretty, and convenient for campers at Goshen Pond Camp.
- Atsion Lake: There is a state campground on one side of the lake and a picnic area on the other. Canoes may be rented at a livery situated on the north bank. The bus service from New York City is convenient.

Batsto River

- Batsto Lake: Medium-sized. Batsto Village is located at the southern end.

Oswego River

- Harrisville Pond: More like a lake than a pond.
- Oswego Lake

Northeast

Toms River

- Colliers Mills Lake
- Success Lake: This lake and Colliers Mills Lake feed the Ridgeway Branch, south of the main branch of the Toms. They lie on a tract that was purchased by the state Division of Fish, Game and Shellfisheries. Both are now part of the Colliers Mills Wildlife Management Area, which is open to hunting and contains a hunter education facility. Success

Lake is accessible only by a gravel road. It is attractive, remote and has more of a wilderness setting than probably any other lake in the Pine Barrens.

Metedeconk River

- Forge Pond: Small but attractive and good for an hour or two of paddling. Canoes may be rented close by at an agency in Brick Town.
- Lake Carasaljo: An attractive lake in the town of Lakewood.
- Lake Shenandoah in Lakewood

Manasquan River

- Turkey Swamp Park: Canoes can be rented for use on the pond. The park contains camping facilities.

Northwest

Rancocas Creek

- Browns Mills Lake

South

Great Egg Harbor River

- New Brooklyn Lake
- Lake Lenape: Canoes may be rented at Mays Landing or at a campground upstream. From the campground you can paddle to the lake and back, viewing the interesting marshy area adjacent to the lake.

Maurice River

- Willow Grove Lake: Very pretty, but parking is limited.
- Union Lake is closed, probably until 1997, to facilitate cleanup of arsenic.

Seldom Paddled Streams

The Pine Barrens are laced with numerous small streams. When several join together, they form the better-known canoe routes which are described in this book. Considered separately, some of these streams are still historically important and very attractive. Under ideal conditions, they may be canoeable. The challenge is to find those streams that are not too overgrown and to try them when the water level is high enough. Most of them are short. In any event, they are definitely not crowded with paddlers on summer weekends.

Exploration of such streams is almost impossible without large-scale maps. Even with good maps, one can expect to get lost in the maze of sand roads throughout the Pinelands. The Hagstrom or Patton maps of Atlantic, Burlington, Camden, Cumberland, Gloucester, Monmouth and Ocean counties are excellent and often more useful than the USGS topographic maps. They are usually available in better bookstores. Another useful aid is the *New Jersey Guide to Wildlife Management Areas*, available at a nominal price from the New Jersey Department of Environmental Protection, Division of Fish, Game and Wildlife, 501 East State Street, CN 400, Trenton, NJ 08625.

Al and Fran Braley explored some streams, learned of others that have been paddled and noted still more: Some of them offer good possibilities for exploration and adventure; others are unlikely to be worthwhile. One should not try any of them without a good day's start and a saw and pruning clippers.

243

What looks like a short run could be a long day (and night) of bushes, brambles, logs and shallow swamp.

Bass River. The Bass River is a tributary of the lower Mullica River, east of Wharton State Forest in Burlington County. Much of its watershed is in Bass River State Forest. Access may be possible at either the West or East Branch, both flowing under Route 653 (Stage Road). The East Branch is the outflow of Lake Absegami. At Route 653 these branches are tiny forest streamlets and heavily overgrown. They join downstream and the next access is about 2 miles south, at the Route 9 drawbridge east of New Gretna, where the river is wide and tidal.

Burrs Mill Brook. Burrs Mill Brook is a tiny, overgrown tributary of another adventure in canoeing, Friendship Creek. It is unlikely to be navigable south of Route 70.

Friendship Creek. This is a small tributary of that portion of the South Branch of the Rancocas that is within the Pine Barrens. It may be canoeable from Route 70, near Leisuretown, to somewhere near Retreat.

Little Ease Run. This stream feeds Willow Grove Lake, the origin of the Maurice River. It flows south out of Gloucester County and defines the northern border between Salem and Cumberland counties. It is accessible at Route 40, west of Malaga, but the river is overgrown all the way to the lake. With good water conditions, however, Little Ease Run may be an attractive alternative to Scotland Run for paddling down the Maurice. Upstream of Route 40, it is probably too narrow.

Manumuskin River. A tributary of the Maurice in Cumberland County that is most likely unexplored. It may be possible to paddle from Bennetts Mill to Cumberland; below that it is tidal.

Manantico Creek. Manantico Creek is a tiny, overgrown tributary of the lower Maurice River, in Cumberland County. It is not likely to be navigable above Route 49, but from there it flows through the Manantico Ponds Wildlife Management Area, where it becomes tidal. In the Wildlife Management Area, it is a maze of pools and interconnecting channels from a restored gravel pit operation. A delightful day can be had by exploring and getting lost in this wilderness of ponds.

Ridgeway Branch of the Toms River. The Ridgeway Branch begins in the Colliers Mills Wildlife Management Area, north of Lakehurst, where it does not appear to be large enough to paddle. Local residents are reported to have run it in high water from Route 547, near the Lakehurst Naval Air Station, to the Toms River. They noted that it is more heavily overgrown than the Toms River. It appears more promising from Route 70 to the Toms River.

Sleeper Branch of the Mullica River. This tributary is parallel to the Nescochague and flows into the Mullica just above Pleasant Mills. Unlike the Nescochague, which has been cleared and is described earlier in this book, the Sleeper is probably too overgrown to paddle. At Route 206 it appears just as obstructed as the initial, uncleared portion of the Albertson Brook tributary to the Nescochague.

South River. This is an unexplored tributary of the Great Egg Harbor River. Possibly it can be paddled either from Route 540 or downstream from Route 552, west of Mays Landing, to Route 50 at Belcoville, where it becomes tidal.

Springers Brook. Springers Brook feeds the Batsto. Don't try it from Route 206, but possibly in high water one can put in at Hampton Furnace Road and continue to the Batsto.

Tuckahoe River. This river is the southernmost of the streams in the Pine Barrens. It runs along the southern and a portion of the western border of Atlantic County. The Lazy River Campground, at the riverbank on Cumberland Avenue about 3 miles west of Estell Manor, suggests the nature of the river. Canoes can be put in here. Maps indicate that downstream of the campground are a number of small lakes, each of which may have a dam that necessitates a carry. Much of this portion of the river flows through Peaslee Wildlife Management Area. On Route 49 west of Head of River, another dam offers good access, and the river looks promising for paddling in the vicinity of Belleplain State Forest. In about 3 miles is yet another dam and access at a second crossing of Route 49, this time east of Head of River. After this the river becomes tidal, and the next access is at the boat ramp in a community park in Corbin City. The tidal section below the park could be interesting to birdwatchers, inasmuch as it flows through the salt marshes of the Lester G. MacNamara Wildlife Management Area, one of the oldest Wildlife Management Areas in the state. It also has a boat ramp.

Tulpehocken Creek. Tulpehocken Creek enters the Wading River after crossing under Hawkin Bridge. The usual access, noted in the river description for the Wading River, is to paddle it upstream from the bridge. However, the creek does cross the Carranza Road east of the Carranza Memorial. Here the creek is a moderate size and flows into a swampy area. In high water it may be navigable.

Upper Oswego River. It forms the southern border of Penn State Forest. Unfortunately, all the roads crossing the stream are private, blocked and barricaded; the only exception is a crossing at Papoose Branch, which is only a trickle. According to reports, one can canoe within 2 or 3 miles of the state forest by paddling upstream from Oswego Lake.

246

Wrangle Branch of the Toms River. Probably a poor candidate for canoeing. It flows through Holiday City, a developed area west of Toms River, before joining the Toms.

Westecunk Creek. A large part of Burlington County's Westecunk Creek lies beneath the several ponds and old cranberry bogs in Stafford Forge Wildlife Management Area, which is currently under development. The ponds do not appear attractive, because of their open and windswept surrounding. The dam for the last pond is under the bridge at Martha Road, just west of the Garden State Parkway; there, the stream begins a 2½-mile run to Railroad Avenue in the town of West Creek. This is the best take-out; the take-out at Route 9 is less appealing and adds only 100 yards to the run. Below Route 9 the creek is tidal and quickly enters Little Egg Harbor. Some clearing of the creek is evident at the entrance to the pool just above Railroad Avenue.

Appendix A

Campgrounds

Alboncondo Camp Grounds
1480 Whitesville Road
Toms River, NJ 08753
(201) 349–4079

Allaire State Park
Box 218
Farmingdale, NJ 07727
(201) 938–2371

Atsion Lake Camp
(see Wharton State Forest)

Bass River State Forest
New Gretna, NJ 08224
(609) 296–2554

Batona Camp
(see Wharton State Forest or Lebanon State Forest)

Bel Haven Lake
R.D. #2
Egg Harbor, NJ 08215
(609) 965–2031, 965–2205

Bodines Field Camp
(see Wharton State Forest)

Buttonwood Hill Camp
(see Wharton State Forest)

Cedar Creek Camp Ground
1052 U.S. Highway No. 9
Bayville, NJ 08721
(201) 269–1413

Godfrey Bridge Camp
(see Wharton State Forest)

Goshen Pond Camp
(see Wharton State Forest)

Hawkin Bridge Camp
(see Wharton State Forest)

Indian Branch Park Campground
U.S. Route 322
Hammonton, NJ 08037
(609) 561–4719

Lebanon State Forest
New Lisbon, NJ 08064
(609) 894–2740

Lower Forge Camp
(see Wharton State Forest)

Mullica River Camp
(see Wharton State Forest)

Paradise Lake Campground
Route 206, P.O. Box 46
Hammonton, NJ 08037
(609) 561–7095

Parvin State Park
R.D. #1
Elmer, NJ 08318
(609) 692–7039

Pine Cone Campground
480 Georgia Road
Freehold, NJ 07728
(201) 462–2230

Riverwood Park
(open 9 A.M. to 4 P.M. Monday through Friday)
Recreation office
Merrimac Drive
Toms River, NJ 08753
(201) 349–4466

Surf and Stream KOA Camp Site
R.D. #3, Box 203
Toms River, NJ 08753
(201) 349–8919

Turkey Swamp Park
Box 86C, Nomoco Road
R.D. #4
Freehold, NJ 07728
(201) 462–7286

Wading Pines Campground
P.O. Box 43
Chatsworth, NJ 08019
(609) 726–1313

Wharton State Forest
For Goshen Pond, Atsion Lake,
Mullica River and Lower Forge camps:

Wharton State Forest
Atsion, R.D. #2
Vincentown, NJ 08088
(609) 268–0444

For any of the camps in the forest:
Wharton State Forest
Batsto, R.D. #4
Hammonton, NJ 08037
(609) 561–0024
561–3262

Winding River Campgrounds
R.D. #2, Box 246
Mays Landing, NJ 08330
(609) 625–3191

Appendix B

Canoe Rental Agencies

All the agencies listed provide transportation to and from the river as an extra service, except where noted; some agencies provide hauling only for groups. Some agencies' locations differ from their mailing addresses. Since most prospective canoeists will want to write ahead for information, the mailing addresses are provided here.

Adams Canoe Rentals
694 Atsion Road, R.D. #2
Vincentown, NJ 08088
(609) 268–0189

Albocondo Camp Grounds
1480 Whitesville Road
Toms River, NJ 08753
(201) 349–4079

Algonquin Adventures
Squankum Road
Farmdale, NJ 07727
(201) 938–7755
899–2916

Art's Canoe Rentals
(Cedar Creek Campground)
Route 9
Bayville, NJ 08721
(201) 269–1413

Bel Haven Lake
R.D. #2
Egg Harbor, NJ 08215
(609) 965–2031
965–2205

Forks Landing Marina
R.D. #1, Box 195
Sweetwater, NJ 08037
(609) 561–4337

Hack's Canoe Retreat
100 Mill Street
Mount Holly, NJ 08060
(609) 267–0116

Lampe's Maurice River Canoe Rental
2580 West Garden Road
Vineland, NJ 08360
(609) 692–8440

Lenape Park Recreation Center
Park Road
Mays Landing, NJ 08330
(609) 625–1191

Micks' Canoe Rental
Route 563, Box 45
Chatsworth, NJ 08019
(609) 726–1380

Mullica River Boat Basin
Route 542
Green Bank, NJ 08215
(609) 965–2120

Paradise Lake Campground
Route 206, P.O. Box 46
Hammonton, NJ 08037
(609) 561–7095

Pine Barrens Canoe Rental
Route 563
Jenkins Post Office
Chatsworth, NJ 08019
(609) 726–1515

Pineland Canoes
632 Carol Fox Road
Brick Town, NJ 08723
(201) 892–8811

Surf and Stream Canoe Rental
KOA Campground
Route 571
Toms River, NJ 08753
(201) 349–8919

Triple T Canoe Livery
Locust Road
Beachwood, NJ 08722
(201) 349–9510

Wading Pines Campground
P.O. Box 43
Chatsworth, NJ 08019
(609) 726–1313

Walt's Sunoco Service
(no hauling but car-top carriers available)
Laurelton Circle
Brick Town, NJ 08723
(201) 892–3785

Winding River Campgrounds
R.D. #2, Box 246
Mays Landing, NJ 08330
(609) 625–3191

Appendix C

Medical Facilities

Freehold:
Freehold Area Hospital
West Main Street
(201) 431–2000

Hammonton:
William B. Kessler Memorial Hospital
Central Avenue and White Horse Pike
(609) 561–6700

Lakewood:
The Paul Kimball Hospital
600 River Avenue
(201) 363–1900

Millville:
Millville Hospital
North High Street
(609) 825–3500

Mount Holly:
Burlington County Memorial Hospital
150 Madison Avenue
(609) 267–0700

Neptune:
Jersey Shore Medical Center—Fitkin Hospital
1945 Corlies Avenue
(201) 775–5500

Toms River:
Community Memorial Hospital
State Highway No. 37
(201) 349–8000

Vineland:
Newcomb Hospital
65 State Street
(609) 691–9000

Appendix D

Additional Useful Addresses

For information on land conservation in New Jersey:

The Nature Conservancy
Eastern Regional Office
294 Washington Street, Room 850
Boston, MA 02108

New Jersey Conservation Foundation
300 Mendham Road
Morristown, NJ 07960

New Jersey Pinelands Commission
P.O. Box 7
New Lisbon, NJ 08064

The State Natural Lands Trust
P. O. Box 1390
Trenton, NJ 08625

To report a river obstruction:

U.S. Army Engineer District, Philadelphia
Attention: Operations Division
U.S. Custom House
Second & Chestnut Street
Philadelphia, PA 19106

For a copy of the state's game compendium
(schedule of the hunting season):

New Jersey Division of Fish and Game
Department of Environmental Protection
P. O. Box 1809
Trenton, NJ 08625

Bibliography

Geology

Lewis, J. Volney, and Kummel, Henry B. *The Geology of New Jersey.* Geologic Series, Bulletin 50, 1914, revised and reprinted by New Jersey Department of Conservation and Economic Development, Trenton, 1940.

Lobeck, Armin K. *Things Maps Don't Tell Us.* Macmillan, 1956.

Richards, Horace G. "The Geological Story of New Jersey." *New Jersey Nature News*, January, 1960, pp. 5-7, 18, 19.

Richards, Horace G. *The Geological History of the New Jersey Pine Barrens.* Bulletin 101, New Jersey Audubon Society, 1960.

Schuberth, Christopher J. *The Geology of New York City and Environs.* Natural History Press, 1968.

Widmer, Kemble. *The Geology and Geography of New Jersey.* New Jersey Historical Series, vol. 19, D. Van Nostrand, 1964.

General Information and Socio-Economic History

Beck, Henry Charlton. *Jersey Genesis: The Story of the Mullica River.* Rutgers University Press, 1963.

Becker, D. W. *Indian Place Names in New Jersey.* Phillips-Campbell Publishing, 1964.

261

Bisbee, Henry H. *Sign Posts: Place Names in History of Burlington County, New Jersey.* Alexia Press, 1971.

Caccia, David A. "Cranberry Harvest." *Natural History* magazine, November, 1969, pp. 54-57.

Harrington, M. R. *Indians of New Jersey: Dickon Among the Lenapes.* Rutgers University Press, 1966.

Kobbe, Gustav. *The New Jersey Coast and Pines.* Short Hills, NJ 1899.

McMahon, William. *South Jersey Towns: History and Legend.* Rutgers University Press, 1973.

McPhee, John. "The People of New Jersey's Pine Barrens." *National Geographic Magazine,* January, 1974, pp. 52-77.

McPhee, John. *The Pine Barrens.* Farrar, Straus & Giroux, 1968.

Pierce, Arthur D. *Iron in the Pines: The Story of New Jersey's Ghost Towns and Bog Iron.* Rutgers University Press, 1957.

Thomas, L. S. *The Pine Barrens of New Jersey.* New Jersey Department of Environmental Protection, Bureau of Parks, P. O. Box 1420, Trenton, NJ 08625; free.

Vivian, N. T. *The New Jersey Devil.* Conservation and Environmental Science Center of Southern New Jersey; unbound.

Zinkin, Vivian. *Study of Place-Names of Ocean County, New Jersey, 1609-1849.* Doctoral dissertation, Columbia University, 1968.

Natural History—Ecology and Checklists

Hand, L. E. and E. E. *Plants of the Batsto Nature Trails.* Four-page checklist, 1968; free at Batsto Village.

Harshberger, John W. *The Vegetation of the New Jersey Pine-Barrens.* Dover Publications, 1970 edition of 1916 work.

McCormick, Jack. *A Vegetation Inventory of Two Watersheds in the New Jersey Pine Barrens.* Doctoral thesis, Rutgers University, 1955.

McCormick, Jack. *The Pine Barrens: A Preliminary Ecological*

Inventory. New Jersey State Museum Report #2, Trenton, 1970.

Plant Life of Wharton State Forest. New Jersey Department of Environmental Protection, Natural Areas Section, P. O. Box 1420, Trenton, NJ 08625, or free at Batsto Village.

Princeton-N.S.F. Cedar Study Group Report. *Study of New Jersey Pine Barrens Cedar Swamps*. Princeton University, 1971.

Robichaud, Beryl, and Buell, Murray F. *Vegetation of New Jersey: A Study of Landscape Diversity*. Rutgers University Press, 1973.

Natural History—Plants

Gleason, H. A. *New Britton & Brown Illustrated Flora of the Northeastern United States & Adjacent Canada*. Three vols., Hafner Press, 1968.

Gleason, H. A. *Plants of the Vicinity of New York*. Hafner Press, 1962.

Petrides, George A. *A Field Guide to Trees & Shrubs*. Houghton Mifflin, 1958.

Peterson, Roger Tory, and McKenney, Margaret A. *A Field Guide to Wildflowers*. Houghton Mifflin, 1968.

Shoemaker, Lois M. *Shrubs and Vines of New Jersey*. New Jersey State Museum Bulletin 10, Trenton, 1965.

Stone, Witmer. *The Plants of Southern New Jersey*. New Jersey State Museum, 1910, reprinted by Quarterman Publications, 1973.

Natural History—Wildlife

Leck, Charles. *The Birds of New Jersey: Their Habits and Habitats*. Rutgers University Press, 1975.

Robbins, Chandler, Bruun, Bertel and Zim, Herbert S. *Birds of North America: A Guide to Field Identification*. Golden Press, 1966.

Canoeing Instruction

Basic Canoeing. American National Red Cross, 17th and D Streets, N.W., Washington, DC 20006; 1965.

Canoeing. Boy Scouts of America, North Brunswick, NJ 08902; 1968.

McNair, Robert. *Basic River Canoeing*. Buck Ridge Ski Club, 32 Dartmouth Circle, Swarthmore, PA 19081; 1968.

Urban, John T. *A White Water Handbook for Canoe and Kayak*. Appalachian Mountain Club, 5 Joy Street, Boston, MA 02108; 1975.

Other Canoeing Guides

Canoeing in New Jersey. New Jersey Department of Community Affairs, 363 West State Street, Trenton, NJ 08625; 1974.

Cawley, Margaret and James. *Exploring the Little Rivers of New Jersey*. Rutgers University Press, 1971.

Meyer, Joan and Bill. *Canoe Trails of the Jersey Shore*. Specialty Press, 1974.

Acknowledgments

In preparing my manuscript, I obtained considerable material on the history and geology of southern New Jersey from the Newark Free Public Library and the New Jersey Historical Society. But numerous individuals helped me, and they deserve thanks. Rochelle Kamsar supplied information from the Ocean County Library and many newspaper clippings. Much of my knowledge of the Pine Barrens in general, and the rivers in particular, resulted from the experiences and curiosity of John Meirs. A. Morton Cooper related the history of the Pinelands Environmental Council. Richard E. Galantowicz described the activities of the New Jersey Conservation Foundation. New Jersey State Geologist Kemble Widmer answered questions about geology, and Louis Hand helped identify plants; any errors in the text were caused by my interpretation of what they stated. Professor Philip Justus of Fairleigh Dickinson University called my attention to a valuable report about cedar swamps. In the New Jersey Department of Environmental Protection, Frank H. Rigg, chief of the Bureau of Parks, and Sydney J. Walker, regional supervisor, furnished material on the state-controlled land in the Pine Barrens. Carter Houck, Emilie Pentz, Walter Espenlaub, Ingeborg Lock and Ludwig Bohler donated miscellaneous information and/or helped scout rivers. Jo Josephson also scouted rivers, contributed to the chapter on geology, smoothed rough edges elsewhere and provided continual encouragement.

I am indebted to the publisher for paying me to spend my weeks paddling the rivers. Harold and Deborah Black, in addition to their usual duty of preparing the manuscript for printing, stored my canoe in their garage, even though it furthered the deterioration of their automobile. Fred Weidner prepared the book's cover and attended to a multiplicity of details—maps, printing, binding—so important to the usefulness and appearance of the book. And Constance Stallings was a bulwark against defeat through her enthusiasm, faith, uncanny ability to locate useful information and skill in making the text readable.

Finally, I am grateful to the New York Chapter of the Appalachian Mountain Club for teaching me how to canoe and for introducing me to the charms of the Pine Barrens.

For the Third Edition

Almost all the revisions in this third edition are based on information supplied by Fran and Al Braley. Some of the necessary updating was possible without their help, but it would not have been complete, and their efforts have enriched the book to an extent that anyone can easily see by comparing this edition to the first.

To correct an oversight, I wish to acknowledge the revision in the second edition by Constance Stallings, who updated to 1981 the continuing conflict between development and preservation of the Pine Barrens. The conflict is still raging, and this third edition reflects the help of Michael Gallaway and Roger Stewart in highlighting current efforts to conserve the Pinelands. I am also grateful to Nina Maurer for her careful editing of this edition.